Ancient Greece: A Very Short Introduction

'Thoroughly stimulating book.'
Tom Holland, *BBC History*

'Cartledge is a master of his subject.'
Peter Joes, *Literary Review*

'A wonderfully concise—and witty—introduction to an ever-popular subject.'
Sir John Boardman, co-editor of *The Oxford History of Greece and the Hellenistic World*

'Paul Cartledge has here pulled off a remarkably clever feat of compression and organization, and will once again place very many readers in his debt. Brilliantly carried through.'
Simon Hornblower, co-editor of *The Oxford Companion to Classical Civilization*

'Telling the grand story of the Ancient Greeks through in-depth portraits of eleven great city-states is a brilliant approach.'
Josiah Ober, Stanford University

VERY SHORT INTRODUCTIONS are for anyone wanting a stimulating and accessible way into a new subject. They are written by experts, and have been translated into more than 45 different languages.

The series began in 1995, and now covers a wide variety of topics in every discipline. The VSI library now contains over 500 volumes—a Very Short Introduction to everything from Psychology and Philosophy of Science to American History and Relativity—and continues to grow in every subject area.

Titles in the series include the following:

Paul Cartledge

ANCIENT GREECE

A Very Short Introduction

OXFORD
UNIVERSITY PRESS

OXFORD

UNIVERSITY PRESS

Great Clarendon Street, Oxford OX2 6DP

Oxford University Press is a department of the University of Oxford.
It furthers the University's objective of excellence in research, scholarship,
and education by publishing worldwide in

Oxford New York

Auckland Cape Town Dar es Salaam Hong Kong Karachi
Kuala Lumpur Madrid Melbourne Mexico City Nairobi
New Delhi Shanghai Taipei Toronto

With offices in

Argentina Austria Brazil Chile Czech Republic France Greece
Guatemala Hungary Italy Japan Poland Portugal Singapore
South Korea Switzerland Thailand Turkey Ukraine Vietnam

Oxford is a registered trade mark of Oxford University Press
in the UK and in certain other countries

Published in the United States
by Oxford University Press Inc., New York

First published in hardback as *Ancient Greece: A History in Eleven Cities* 2009
First published as a *Very Short Introduction* 2011

British Library Cataloguing in Publication Data

Data available

Library of Congress Cataloging in Publication Data

Data available

Typeset by SPI Publisher Services, Pondicherry, India
Printed in Great Britain on acid-free paper by
Ashford Colour Press Ltd., Gosport, Hampshire.

ISBN 978-0-19-960134-9

14

Preface

It is very hard, in a short book, to do anything like full justice to an 'Ancient Greece' that was a conglomerated civilization or culture of roughly 1,000 separate and often very distinct political entities at any one moment in ancient time, and that stretched at the limit from southern Spain to the Black Sea shore of modern Georgia. (The Fitzwilliam Museum in Cambridge in 2008 hosted an exhibition devoted to splendidly sophisticated, mainly Greek-made finds from graves in Vani, Georgia, associated with an in-house exhibition of coins from the Black Sea region generally.)

A Who's Who, a Glossary, and a Chronology have been included to enhance ease of quick reference, together with notes on the spelling of Greek words and names, and on Greek measures of money and distance. But I should also like to draw readers' attention to *The Cambridge Illustrated History of Ancient Greece*. Like this book, the *CIHAG* combines thematic with chronological approaches, and social, economic, religious, and cultural with political, military, and diplomatic history, but in a format which, unlike the present volume, is very definitely not suitable for pulling out of a pocket to read on the train or bus or plane. I hope that it may be useful as a companion to readers of this book, as it has been to me in the writing of it.

Acknowledgements

I should like to thank again my collaborators on *The Cambridge History of Ancient Greece*: Sue Alcock (now of Brown University), Nick Fisher (University of Wales, Cardiff), Marilyn Katz (Wesleyan University), Edith Hall (now Royal Holloway University of London), Karim Arafat (King's College London), Catherine Morgan (now Director of the British School at Athens), Lesley Dean-Jones (University of Texas at Austin), and Richard Buxton (Bristol University); and the other colleagues and friends, too, on the continent of Europe (especially in Greece), in Africa, in America North and South, in Australasia, and in Japan, who have in some way or other contributed to the text that follows. There are too many to name them all individually, but two do require special mention: Robert Garland (Colgate University) and Polly Low (University of Manchester), who both at extremely short notice read and commented expertly on an entire near-final draft. And I must not forget the Press's 'anonymous reader', who saved me from considerable embarrassment. Were it not for their kindness and collegiality, this book would have been even more imperfect than it is. I count myself exceedingly fortunate, too, to be writing at a time when the modern historiography of ancient Greece is experiencing something of a boom, and, not least, when outreach to wider publics than just one's fellow-specialists is considered a (pleasurable) duty rather than a luxury.

It is in that same spirit of striving for outreach that I was deeply honoured to have my personal chair in Cambridge's Faculty of Classics endowed in perpetuity as the A. G. Leventis Professorship of Greek Culture (with effect from 1 October 2008). This book is one of the first fruits of that charity, and it is dedicated, in a spirit of ineffable *kharis*, to the Trustees of the A. G. Leventis Foundation.

Contents

Note on spelling of Greek names/words

By inclination I prefer to transliterate rather than anglicize ancient Greek names and words, but even I write Aeschylus and Thucydides, not Aiskhulos and Thoukudides. Here I have deviated from strict transliteration in various, not always consistent ways—a truly British compromise (or muddle): thus, for example, Cnossos, not Knossos (transliteration), nor Cnossus (Latin). But one outstanding exception had to be made—for Byzantion (the city); this in order to avoid confusion with anglicized, Latinate Byzantium (either a civilization or an epoch—during which 'Byzantion', as the city-name, 'got the works' in favour of 'Konstantinoupolis'—Constantinople). Where I place a circumflex over the 'e' or 'o' of a transliterated ancient Greek word, that is to indicate, especially in cases where transliteration might lead to misunderstanding, that the vowel was long—or 'big' as the Greeks said: *omicron* = (literally) small 'o', *ômega* = big 'o'. Greek short 'e', *epsilon*, meant 'light "e"'; the long version was called 'êta'.

Greek measures of money and distance

I. Money

> 6 obols = 1 drachma
> 2 drachmas = 1 statêr (literally 'balance')
> 100 drachmas = 1 mina (or mna) [the word is of
> Babylonian origin]
> 60 minas = 1 talent [also of Babylonian origin]

Note, first, that the value of coins—struck in electrum, gold, silver, or bronze, from the later seventh century on—was a function of their weight, and that different cities operated different weight-standards, often those established by another city. Second, although it is not possible straightforwardly to translate ancient weights/values into modern currency equivalents, it may be helpful to bear in mind that the average rate of daily pay for a skilled craftsman varied during the fifth and fourth centuries BCE between 1 and 2.5 drachmas, and that rough parity was established between a daily craftsman's wage-rate and the pay given by democratic Athens to citizens for attendance at the Assembly between the 390s and 320s. The daily cost of living for a family of four in Athens at the end of the fifth century is estimated at between 2.5 and 6 obols. Third, small change—fractions of silver obols—was in use by the end of the sixth century, struck by mints including those of Colophon, Aegina, Mende, and Abdera; it could be offered as payment for pots, legal fines, or fees for initiation into a religious cult. Much less valuable bronze coinage was not struck in quantity until the end of the fifth century, by which time an issue of gold coinage by a Greek city signified emergency—in sharp contrast to the Persian empire, where it constituted business as usual, and a powerful diplomatic as well as commercial instrument.

II. Distance

1 *stadion* = 600 'feet' or roughly 200 metres (in practice, normally rather less; e.g. at Olympia about 192 metres).
Again, note that different cities calculated the basic 'foot' differently.

List of illustrations

List of maps

Map 1. Greece & the Aegean World

Chapter 1
Introduction

The polis *is the Greek version of the city-state, and the network of more than 1,000* poleis *constitutes the largest city-state culture in world history, both geographically and demographically.*

(Mogens Herman Hansen, *Polis*, 146)

The principal aim of this short book (a breviarium not an epitome) is to provide a fairly painless and highly stimulating introduction to the complex, diverse, and challenging subject of the history of ancient Greek civilization, without being either simplistic or bland. I understand Greek history and civilization in very broad ethnic and chronological senses, from the first documented use of the Greek language in about 1400 BCE at Cnossos down to the foundation of the (post-Ancient, as I see it here) Byzantine empire based on Constantinople (formerly Byzantion) in about CE 330.

To make some sense of such a huge world (from the Black Sea to Spain) and such a vast expanse of time, within the scope of a short volume, I have written the book around eleven major Greek cities, the histories of which can be variously used to illuminate what I take to be the most important and informative Hellenic themes:

1

politics, trade, travel, slavery, gender, religion, philosophy, historiography, and the role of prominent individuals, among others. In the process of exposition I shall pay due attention also to how the (any) history of ancient Greece is constructed: that is, to what the nature of the available evidence—contemporary or non-contemporary, written or non-written, and so forth—is; and how professional scholars and other writers have used, or could or should best use, that evidence.

If called to specify 'Ancient Greece' further, I would analyse it as a civilization of cities. The English word 'civilization' is derived ultimately from Latin *civitas*, community, from which comes also our 'city'. But the Romans were not the first to develop a civilization of cities, a 'citification' of culture. There the Greeks, along with the Etruscans in Italy and the Phoenicians of modern Lebanon, preceded them. Indeed, on a looser definition of 'city' it is possible to trace the origins of civilization in the sense of citification as far back as the third or fourth millennium BCE, to the 'inter-riverine' civilizations of lower and upper Mesopotamia (modern Iraq). But here I wish to give 'city' a qualitative as well as quantitative connotation, implying a type of self-governing geopolitical space combining town and country in a dynamic symbiosis.

Today it is estimated that on some definition of 'city' more than half the world's population live in one. Indeed, a few mega-cities—Tokyo, New York—have a GDP similar in size to that of whole countries (Spain, Canada)... In my ancient Greek world, in the sharpest possible contrast, as many as 90 per cent of the population may have lived regularly and normally in the countryside as opposed to any space that may properly be labelled urban. Put it the other way round: not all Greeks by any means lived in cities; even in the heavily urbanized Athens of the later fifth century most Athenians still lived in the countryside, as Thucydides relates. And yet—and this explains my decision to work with and through eleven Greek cities—the characteristic, defining mode of Hellenic social coexistence was, for ten out of the fourteen or so centuries covered here, what the Greeks called a *polis*. As Aristotle famously stipulated in his *Politics* ('Matters relating to the *polis*'), man—humankind—is a 'political animal', in the precise sense of a living organism designed by its nature to fulfil its potential within and only within the *polis* political framework.

Actually, *polis* is one of the most frequently attested nouns in ancient Greek, ranking 39th in a list of the 2,000 most common Greek words, ahead of such nouns as *anêr* (man in the gender sense) and *theos* (god). It could have as many as four different meanings, of which two—city (*qua* urban central space) and state—are the most important for us. For what counts for my project is that, even though a majority lived in towns or villages (in the *khôra* or countryside) rather than cities or urban centres, the free adult male citizens, the event-making movers and shakers of ancient Hellenism, were full sharing members of political communities also called *polis*—for which the best translation into English is 'citizen-state'. And it was in the urban centre, the city in its narrower political sense, that collective self-government found decisive expression. It is from the ancient Greek *polis* in that sense that we derive 'politics' and its cognates, and it is this feature of Greek civilization, which spawned such key terms as aristocracy, oligarchy, tyranny and—last but by no means least—democracy, that gives ancient Greece much of its enduring and current salience.

It is important to be clear from the outset that there never was anything like an ancient equivalent of a nation-state of 'Greece', but only, as we shall see, a network of Greek cities and other kinds of settlements bound together by a sense of common culture expressed importantly through what we would call religious means. Herodotus, Greece's and the world's first historian properly so-called, placed the following definition of 'Greekness' in the mouths of his Athenian speakers, addressing the Spartans, their

3

allies, at a crucial moment of the decisive conflict between Greeks and 'barbarian' (non-Greek) Persians during the winter of 480/479 BCE:

> ... it would not be fitting for the Athenians to prove traitors to the Greek people, with whom we are united in sharing the same kinship and language, with whom we have established shrines and conduct sacrifices to the gods together, and with whom we also share the same way of life.
>
> (*Histories*, Book 8, chapter 144, in the translation of Andrea Purvis)

The words are invented by Herodotus, and they imply an agreed unity that was only very rarely realized in common political as opposed to cultural action. The telling absence of any reference to political unity in this persuasive definition of a 'pan-Hellenic' (all-Greek) identity speaks loudly. Indeed, it is arguable that it was precisely the absence of a nation-state or, to put that positively, the highly individualistic nature of the Greek *polis*, that gives Greek civilization its unique identity. Just why the different Greek *poleis* emerged, or were created, and how they differed from earlier cities, will be tackled more specifically in the particular chapters that follow.

At any one time during the last half of the first millennium BCE and the first three centuries CE about 1,000 or so separate entities existed that could claim the appellation of *polis*. We know this and can state it with confidence, thanks to the decade-long researches of the 'Copenhagen Polis Centre' directed inimitably by Mogens Herman Hansen. The choice of just eleven out of those 1,000 required the judgement of Rhadamanthys (son of Zeus and Europa, brother of Minos: see Chapter 2). Various factors and motives came into play. I wanted to include an island city—either a city on a Greek island or a city that was also the sole *polis* of a Greek island; I ended up with Cnossos on the island of Crete. I wanted the major regional divisions of the Aegean Greek heartland or Hellenic core area to be represented: hence three

4

cities of the 'island of Pelops' or Peloponnese (Mycenae, Argos, and Sparta), two from Central Greece (Athens and Thebes), one from 'East Greece', that is the western littoral of Anatolia or 'Asia Minor' as it used to be known (Miletus), and one spanning east and west, the Eurasian city of Byzantion (later Constantinople, now Istanbul). Next, it was vital that the Greek 'colonial' diaspora be represented properly—hence the selection of Massalia, now Marseilles (founded from an East Greek city), Syracuse (founded from a Peloponnesian city), and Byzantion (founded from a central Greek city); actually, they were not really 'colonies' in our sense (the Greek *apoikia* simply meant 'home from home'), but the terminology is conventional. Finally, I needed a representative of the new, post-Classical 'Hellenistic' world created by Alexander the Great's conquests and celebrated in the late nineteenth and early twentieth centuries by my favourite modern Greek poet, C. P. Cavafy—so, what better choice could there be than Cavafy's own native city, Alexandria in Egypt, founded for sure (as a number of other 'Alexandrias' were not certainly) by Alexander himself?

Of course, I have my regrets, as will my readers no doubt: why none from mainland Greece north of Thebes (Protagoras's and Democritus's Abdera, for instance)? or from the Black Sea region (Olbia, say), or from north Africa west of Alexandria, in today's Libya (Cyrene is the obvious candidate)? Why not other (different) ones from the Peloponnese—Corinth, perhaps, or Messene or Megalopolis? The list could be extended, and there were various reasons for my exclusions—above all, lack of good or at least good and fairly continuous contemporary authentic evidence. But at least one of the above cities, Corinth, does get its day in the sun, as the founding city of Syracuse; and I shall hope to compensate for at least some others of these enforced absences and silences in stimulatingly alternative ways.

Chapter 2
Cnossos

And every time, it is ships, it is ships, it is ships of Cnossos coming...

(From D. H. Lawrence, 'The Greeks are Coming')

In 2008 the Alexander S. Onassis Public Benefit Foundation (USA) staged a typically handsome and informative exhibition in their headquarters in midtown Manhattan, which they entitled 'The First Palatial Civilization in Europe: Minoan Crete, 3000–1100 BC'. The more than 200 objects on display were arresting enough—wall-painting fragments, precious jewellery and figurines in various materials, ceremonial vessels and offerings, sealstones, pottery, tools, traces of food preparation, and inscribed tablets. Indeed, it is the last item in that list, the 3,000–4,000 tablets inscribed in the 'Linear B' syllabic script found in the palace at Cnossos and datable to around 1400 BCE, that has earned the city of Cnossos pole position on our starting-grid of Greek cities. For in 1952 the architect and amateur codebreaker Michael Ventris, indispensably assisted by the Cambridge Hellenist John Chadwick, announced to an astonished world that Linear B—unlike its Cretan predecessor, the still undeciphered Linear A script—had been devised to transcribe the earliest known form of the Greek language (and not, for instance, Etruscan—still undeciphered...). Ventris and Chadwick thus added more than half a millennium to the language's known history, and gave an entirely new meaning to what—from a historian's viewpoint—is the latest stage of Greek prehistory, in archaeologists' parlance the Late Bronze Age.

Almost as exciting, though, was the exhibition's title, which with a truly Greek passion for 'famous firsts' broadly and loosely designated the Cretan Early, Middle, and Late Bronze Ages as 'the first palatial civilization in Europe'. Actually, Crete is an island distinguished in important part precisely because it is not geographically on the European continental mainland but lies roughly equidistant between southern Greece and north Africa, and athwart trading and migration routes running from the eastern Mediterranean (the Near or Middle East today) to Greece, Egypt, and points further west. Aptly, its fauna and flora and microclimates exactly reproduce the island's median position between the three continents of Europe, Africa, and Asia, making it one of the most fascinating of all the contiguously bounded Greek terrains for the tourist to visit today.

That the Cretan Bronze Age was a 'palatial' civilization is not controversial, though the first palaces—at Cnossos and four other centres extending across the island's 160-kilometre length (it is the fourth largest island in the Mediterranean after Cyprus, Sicily, and Sardinia)—were developed much nearer 2000 than 3000 BCE. But that the civilization was ever Greek at all in any sense was proven only by Ventris and Chadwick, half a century and more after (Sir) Arthur Evans (1851–1941), pioneer excavator of Cnossos, had dubbed it 'Minoan' in honour of a Cretan King Minos of much later Greek legend. Herodotus, fully earning his spurs as the world's first historian, had very sensibly doubted whether a Minos had ever really existed, since he did not belong to the 'so-called human generation', as opposed to the pre-human world of myth and legend. But Evans was not only hugely wealthy and a fiercely competitive and energetic excavator, but also a gifted publicist, and his 'Minoan' tag served both to humanize and to hellenize a culture that was not only pre-Greek in origin but also

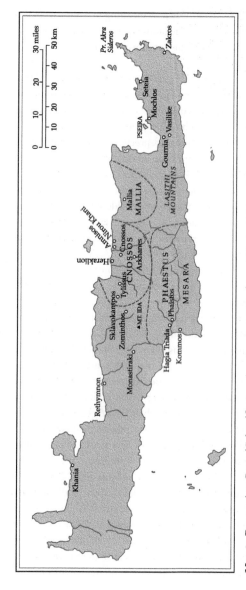

Map 2. Bronze Age Crete (*Scientific American* 'Ancient Cities' special issue 1994, p. 48)

for most of its duration un-Greek. For, whatever language 'Linear A' script may record, it is certainly not Greek—and possibly belongs, not to the Indo-European language family of which Greek is a member, but to the Semitic language family. Most later Greeks of the historical period—Herodotus being a major exception—were convinced that the legendary eponym Minos was as real and as Greek as could be; indeed, he was thought to have functioned in the emblematic manner of early rulers, as a lawgiver. This was appropriate enough, in one way, since historic-era Crete with its reputed one hundred cities (in fact far fewer) was famously fertile in producing legislators and laws. The best-known are those of the central Cretan city of Gortyn (below). But we today should be very wary of leaping to infer that Evans's—and the ancient Greeks'—Minos was a real-life, proto-Greek counterpart of the utterly real Babylonian codemaker Hammurabi (early eighteenth century BCE).

The true interest of Minos is that he is a character from one of the ancient Greeks' most enduring intellectual and performative inventions, namely myth. It is true that some myths—'tales' is what the Greek word *muthoi* generically means, traditional ones in this particular case—may contain historical matter buried somewhere deep down near their origins. But it is not for their correspondence to historical fact that traditional tales become myths and serve the various functions—explanation of the world's composition and creation, or legitimation of political power, for example—that myths definitionally perform. Myths' practical functions normally far outweigh their (usually scant or null) verifiably accurate historical content. Thus, although the compilers of a Greek chronography known as the Parian Marble (written up on local stone on the Cycladic island of Paros in the late 260s BCE) included the reign of Minos in their listing of 'Greek History' dates between (what we call) 1582 and 264/3 BCE, we would do far better to stick with the scepticism noted above of Herodotus, and regard Minos (product of the rape by Zeus in the guise of a bull of the Phoenician princess Europê) and his alleged

9

thalassocracy as no more historical and no less mythical than the Minotaur (offspring of Minos's wife Pasiphae and—the recurring bovine motif obtrudes—a bull).

At best, then, we may speak of 'myth-history', as far as the Late Bronze Age of Crete is concerned—and that goes for the rest of Greece too (despite the ostensible historicity of the Homeric poems, as we shall see in the next chapter). That myth-history, supplemented or corrected by the mute but usually objective data of archaeology, is indeed all we have to go on for reconstructing at least the first seven or so centuries (c.1500–800 BCE) of attested Greek activity. And the first observation to be made is of difference. That is, between the world of the prehistoric Greek or non-Greek palace and the historic Greek *polis* there is a fixed and unbridgeable gulf—a gulf in both material and ideological as well as more narrowly political culture.

The Cretan Late Bronze Age palace—Cnossos's measured some 750 square metres in area—functioned politically and ceremonially as the seat and symbol of power exercised by some sort of paramount chief or overlord, a 'big man' (presumably, rather than a Queen) who—at least under the Greek dispensation—may have been called *anax* or 'lord'. But there were other people of distinction and consequence, inhabiting close by what have been called 'mansions' constructed of the same finely dressed and neatly jointed ashlar masonry as the palace itself. Economically, the palace of Cnossos acted as a redistributive and storage centre capable, it is most recently thought, of supporting some 14,000–18,000 souls (a sober estimate far more plausible than the grossly inflated figure of 80,000–100,000 favoured by Evans himself).

At the core of this fundamentally agrarian regime, and made possible by a climate which seems in essentials to have changed but little over three thousand years, was the 'Mediterranean triad' of dietary staples: grain (chiefly barley, because it is much more drought-resistant, but also various kinds of wheat and some other lesser grains such as millet), wine (Cretan soil and climate still are famously suitable for viticulture), and oil, that is, olive oil (ditto). It is estimated from the storage capacity of the jars in the palace's west wing that to fill them might have required as many as 32,000 olive trees grown on an area of 320 hectares. But these three staples were powerfully supplemented by coriander and saffron and—at least to judge from the later Linear B tablets—by serious pasturage of sheep for woolmaking. And the domestic productive economy was interlocked with a sophisticated network of trading contacts extending into Egypt in the south, to the Cyclades islands and southern Peloponnesian mainland to the north, and to the Levant, mediated by a complex system of weights and boosted by the extreme skill of Cretan craftsmen, nowhere displayed to more telling effect than in the production of tiny seals, semi-precious stones, and gold rings engraved with scenes both of everyday life and of religious ritual activity.

The staples triad had been established as such in mutual symbiosis during the Early Bronze Age (third-millennium) 'emergence of civilization' (to use Colin Renfrew's handy but somewhat elliptical phrase). It is tempting therefore, if by 'civilization' we understand citi-fication, to speak of Cnossos as becoming a 'city' of sorts some time around or after 2000 BCE. Strikingly absent, however, not only from Cnossos but from all the other contemporary Cretan palaces and other major settlement centres, are city walls. Comparatively speaking, what is most striking is the absence from Crete of the sort of massive fortification walls that marked—and marked out—the Greek mainland at this time. These walls were known to the later Greeks as 'Cyclopean', because they thought only giants like Homer's one-eyed Cyclopes could possibly have made them.

Not that the palaeo-Cretans were innocent of all aggression, no doubt, let alone bloodshed. Examples of what look uncannily like human sacrifices have been found in eastern Crete and not far from Cnossos itself. But leaving aside such spectacularly gory exceptions, the Late Bronze Age Cretans' establishment of some sort of network of 'colonies' or at least trading outposts stretching from the Aegean to Egypt, such as that at Kastri on the small offshore island of Cythera, is unlikely to have been achieved totally peacefully. Indeed, famous frescoes from the ancient Greek 'Pompeii'—modern Akrotiri on the Cycladic island of Santorini (ancient Thera)—that are datable to before that island's massive volcanic self-destruction in the 1620s BCE show what must surely be 'Minoan' warfleets in action. But back at home, in Crete and especially Cnossos, the most violent kind of licensed social activity seems to have been a form of ritual bull-leaping—leaping, not Spanish-style killing, as is depicted with immense skill in a variety of artistic media, again including fresco. A fine gold cup deposited in a large grave at Vapheio in the south-east Peloponnese dated *c*.1500 seems to show bulls being rounded up for this purpose. On this evidence, it would be rash to deny that there was some form of bull-worship practised on Crete, involving the ceremonial placing and no doubt use for worship of what archaeologists call 'horns of consecration'.

It is against the backdrop of apparent pacificity (if I may coin that word) that the violence of the transition from native Cretan to foreign rule at Cnossos in the period around 1450 BCE transpires so markedly, attested, for conspicuous instance, by the sudden unannounced presence of a number of 'warrior graves' (graves stuffed with—bronze—weapons). What is now known as 'Final Palatial Crete' is thus most economically explained as having been midwifed by conquest, and it is a further economy of inference—from the language and script of the Linear B tablets—to suppose that the invading conquerors were Greek-speakers from the Greek mainland, especially the Peloponnese.

It is true that there has been huge debate over the dating of the Cnossos Linear B tablets. Although Evans did pay some considerable attention to the then newfangled notion of stratigraphy, his encouragement of his workers' speed of work by means of bribery did not lend itself to the most scrupulous recording of levels of deposit, or enable easy retrospective decipherment of the data retrieved from the soil in stratified sequences. In the 1960s my own former Oxford doctoral supervisor, John Boardman, was obliged to defend fiercely the scholarship—and honour—of Evans (who had dated them *c*.1400 BCE) against a determined assault by the philologist L. R. Palmer, who wished to downdate them to *c*.1200 (the rough date of all the other known examples, both from the Greek mainland and from elsewhere in Crete). The Boardman defence of Evans has been universally adjudged successful, more successful at any rate by far than Cnossos's of itself against the mainlanders.

These mainlanders are known to scholarship if not to history as the Mycenaeans, and they will be the subject of the next chapter. But first a brief Cnossian prospect. Cnossos's—and Crete's—political heyday fell in the firmly prehistoric Bronze Age, but Dark Age and Archaic Crete (eleventh to ninth centuries, seventh to sixth centuries) were not a total cultural blank by any means, and the island traditionally was unusually fertile in the creation of early *poleis*. Another tradition, however, is better based and corroborated, namely that of early historical Crete as a land of lawgivers and laws. For conspicuous example, the excavated Agora (see Glossary) of Drerus and a late-seventh-century law inscribed on bronze from that same small city in eastern Crete bear objective witness in support of that claim.

In later historical times Cnossos was revived as a Hellenic city, with an important cult of the earth-mother goddess Demeter. Among the relatively large number of inscribed Cretan documents of the fifth century—most famously, the 'Code' of Gortyn in central Crete, inscribed on temple walls around 450 BCE—there is a fragmentary text of about the same date from the sanctuary of Artemis at Tylissus that links Cnossos with not only Tylissus but also Argos in the Peloponnese (subject of our Chapter 4) in a detailed and complex religious-cum-political pact concerning among other things distribution of war-booty. One possible explanation for the involvement of Argos is that the city was regarded as—and maybe really was—the colonial founder of the other two some time during the Dark Age of the eleventh to tenth centuries, by which time Argos was a Dorian city. At any rate, as an anachronistic reference in Homer had already announced, by the Classical period Crete had been re-colonized, this time by a wave of predominantly Doric-Greek-speaking immigrants (not necessarily also conquerors) who came to stay.

The subsequent fortunes of Cnossos may be traced well into the era of Roman conquest, occupation, and provincialization of the island (after 146 BCE). There has even been talk of a (Roman) 'imperial renaissance'. But what visitors to the site today will see—an 'opera set on a wet afternoon', as I have heard it described—is very much a product of Sir Arthur Evans's imagination.

Chapter 3
Mycenae

*They stick masks on our face, of tragedy or comedy. We have
no mirrors to see ourselves in.*

(From Oktay Rifat's *Agamemnon I*, translated from the
Turkish by Richard McKane and Ruth Christie)

'I gazed on the face of Agamemnon'—so runs the abbreviated
headline-grabbing version of a message telegraphed in November
1876 by an overexcited and deeply mistaken Heinrich Schliemann,
self-made Prussian multimillionaire businessman turned
self-made 'excavator', to a Greek newspaper. For an amateur
driven by the ambition to find the real-life counterparts of
Homer's characters the identification was not just seductively
tempting but inescapable. For the Mycenae of Homer's epic *Iliad*
was adorned with the personalized, formulaic epithet 'rich in gold',
and Agamemnon was the great High King of Mycenae, by far the
most powerful of the regal lords who banded together to rescue
the errant wife of Agamemnon's brother Menelaus from the
adulterously fey clutches of Paris (also known as Alexander), a
prince of the royal house of Troy. Schliemann had of course
already dug there too, indeed could rightly claim to have found at
Hissarlik overlooking the Dardanelles on the Asiatic side the only
possible site of Homer's Troy—if indeed there ever was a precise
and uniform, real-world original of that fabled 'windy' city. But
what he and his team of Greek workmen had in fact discovered at

Mycenae, in one of the six hyper-rich shaft-graves enclosed within a much later (*c.*1300 BCE) city-wall, was a handsome death-mask of a neatly bearded, compactly expressive adult male datable *c.*1650 BCE, well before any sort of Homeric Trojan War could possibly have taken place.

More soberly, accurately, and professionally, if also just a little romantically, Mycenae is the major Late Bronze Age city in the Argolis region of the north-east Peloponnese that has given its name to an entire era: the 'Mycenaean' Age. This is thanks to a combination of archaeology and Homer, mainly the former. As we have seen, archaeology and philology between them tell us that in about 1450 BCE Cnossos was overwhelmed by Greek-speaking invaders from the north. These warrior communities had evolved a culture based, like that of Late Bronze Age Crete, on palaces. But whereas the 'Minoan' culture looks to have been strikingly peaceful or at least internally harmonious, the palace-based rulers of Mycenae and other mainland Mycenaean centres north and south of the Corinthian isthmus (Thebes, Iolcus, Pylus) were notably bellicose and liked to surround themselves with huge walls (those of Mycenae were over 6 metres thick). Whether or not the rulers themselves were literate, they had their archives kept for them in the primitive bureaucratic form of Greek script known prosaically as Linear B (deciphered as Greek as recently as 1952: see previous chapter). The well-known publishing house of Thames & Hudson once included 'The Mycenaeans' in their 'Ancient Peoples and Places' series (an accessible study by Lord William Taylour). But the Mycenaeans were not a 'people' in any authentic, organic, anciently attested sense.

Moreover, though Greek in language, the civilization of Mycenaean Greece was in most other, basic respects a provincial outpost of a Middle Eastern culture whose epicentres lay in Egypt, Syria, and Iraq. The imposing Lion Gate entrance to the citadel recalls Hattusas of the Hittites or even Babylon; and the beehive, corbelled, drystone tombs known as the Treasury of Atreus

(Agamemnon's father) and the Tomb of Aegisthus (lover of Agamemnon's wife Clytemnestra) betray an almost Egyptian lust for imposing posthumous longevity. Palace-frescoes suggest that the buildings rang to the chants of court-musicians, and so, conceivably, there may have been Mycenaean court-poets or at any rate court-lyricists. But the Linear B texts deciphered thus far at least (from Thebes, Tiryns, Ayios Vasilios, and Pylus as well as Mycenae on the mainland, and from Cnossos and Khania, ancient Cydonia, on Crete) contain not a shred of poetry nor any other kind of literature, and, given their documentary, bureaucratic function as temporary records of economic data mainly for tax-purposes, are hardly likely to yield such in the future. (It is, not incidentally, by accident not design that the Linear B tablets were preserved: the fires that consumed the palaces at Mycenae and elsewhere in *c*.1200 BCE baked them to an imperishable hardness.)

In short, Mycenaean culture and society represented, in Hellenic retrospect, a false start. Ironically, in a way, the best possible witness to the gulf between the world of the palace and that of the *polis* are the very epic poems—the *Iliad*, the *Odyssey*, and some others collectively known as the 'epic cycle'—that have been cited to prove the relationship of direct, unbroken, civilizational descent. Ostensibly, indeed, the epics do purport to describe a long-lost, far superior civilization of the sort that the visible remains of Mycenae and other Late Bronze Age capitals evoked. Yet what Greek audiences of the eighth and seventh centuries BCE—the era, that is, when the epics achieved their finished, monumental form—imagined to be colossally huge palace establishments paled by comparison with the real thing, as that was revealed by means inaccessible to the Greeks, namely archaeology, art-history, and linguistics. For example, Homer's audiences were assumed to think of fifty slaves as a suitably vast holding for a heroic king of yore, when actually a Mycenaean palace of the thirteenth century BCE had been able to command the forced labour of hundreds if not thousands of *do-er-oi* (the Mycenaean version of classical Greek *douloi*, meaning 'slaves').

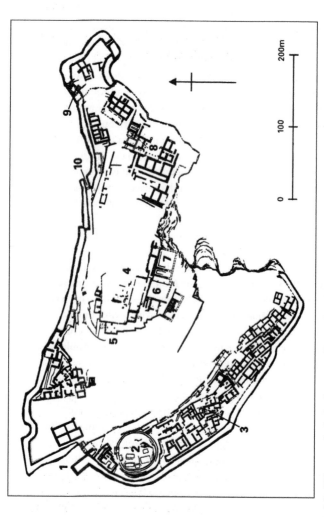

1. Citadel of Mycenae (principal excavated structures): C. Gere, *Tomb of Agamemnon* (Profile, 2006) 182–3. Key: 1 Lion Gate 2 Grave Circle A 3 Cult centre 4 Palace 5 Palace entrance 6 Court 7 Megaron 8 House of Columns 9 Cistern 10 Postern gate

18

And, as noted in the previous chapter, later Greeks could not believe that Mycenae's massive walls had been constructed by mere, ordinary mortals.

This is not of course to deny all cultural continuity between Mycenaean and historical Greece: crucially, the names of several members of the Olympian pantheon occur already in the Linear B tablets, and historical Greek myth unerringly focused its imaginings on major Mycenaean centres. But Mycenaean palace-religion was a far cry from historical Greek temple-religion. For a start, there were no actual temples of Athena like the one imagined in the *Iliad* to have stood at Troy before the late ninth century at the earliest. The roots—ideological as well as physical—of that cardinal structure (*naos* in Greek; a shrine or sanctuary was *hieron*) can be traced back no further than the twelfth century BCE, whereas in Mycenaean Mycenae, as it were, the palatial cult-centre was more akin to a private chapel in an English great house of the early modern era than to a public religious space serving an entire community. (On a tasting note: it would appear from scientific analysis of organic remains found in a large jar from the Room with the Fresco in that intramural palatial cult-centre that the celebrants drank their wine flavoured with pine resin, even as a proto-*retsina* perhaps.)

Nor has archaeology anything like proven, as yet, that anything much like a ten-year siege of non-Greek Troy by a coalition of mainland and island Greeks under a high king of Mycenae really occurred—for all that Hissarlik, the site of an important Anatolian city on the Hellespont (Dardanelles), with links as far east as the mighty Hittite empire in the thirteenth century, is undoubtedly Homer's Troy, the focal point onto which Homeric Greek imaginings were projected. Likewise, the idea of a grand military coalition of Greeks corresponds to precisely what Greeks between about 1200 and 700 BCE could not possibly have achieved—indeed, never actually achieved at any time in their real history, not even under Alexander the Great. It has been well said that the creation of epic and saga presupposes the ruin of an earlier civilization, but that does not mean that the new artistic creation will be a historically faithful copy or mirror of its supposed original. It has also been very well said that the world of Homer is immortal precisely because it never existed as such outside the fertile imaginations of the extended succession of poets who over those five long centuries between about 1200 and 700 BCE created and elaborated a formulaic oral tradition, and then—was this the achievement of a single poet of genius later known as Homer? or of two such, conflated?—crystallized elements of that diverse and redundant tradition in two incomparable, narratively focused monumental epics. As many as seven Greek cities later claimed Homer as a favourite native son; all that is virtually certain is that he—or they—will have hailed from the East Greek culture-area. For it was from here that the artificial Homeric dialect—one never spoken outside the context of an epic recitation—drew the largest portion of its wellsprings, namely the Ionic dialect of Greek (to which we shall come back in Chapter 5).

To return from fiction to fact, round about 1200 BCE the wealthy centres of Mycenaean Greek civilization came cataclysmically crashing down (the doubtless multiple causes are still disputed). There ensued from the eleventh century to the ninth BCE something of a Greek 'Dark' age, dark to us not least because it was illiterate (except on Cyprus, where a descendant of Linear B syllabic script was deployed), but also dark objectively speaking, in the sense that there were many fewer settlements, with much smaller populations, more widely scattered and technologically impoverished. Of course, there are isolated exceptions, Lefkandi on the island of Euboea being among the most notable; and one harbinger of a brighter future was the beginning of the switch from bronze to iron for crucial classes of edged implements. But darkness generally ruled. The Linear B script itself perished along with the hierarchical sociopolitical structure to which it had been symbiotically attached. Mycenae itself, like Cnossos, survived physically into the historical period, despite more than one phase of destruction, but it did so only as a shadowy avatar of its Bronze Age progenitor. The lower town of contemporary Tiryns, not far away from both Mycenae and Argos (Chapter 4), happens to preserve the shabby and poky habitational remains of this twilight postpalatial era rather better than does Mycenae itself.

We today may find the might of Mycenae in its Homeric re-imagining very impressive, but pity the poor Mycenaeans, the historical inhabitants of the city of post-Bronze Age historical Mycenae, listening to endless epic recitations and ever vainly hoping that a little of Agamemnon's aura would rub off on them if only they worshipped hard and often enough at the Agamemnoneion, the historical shrine of the heroized Agamemnon, or at the sanctuary dedicated to another figure of myth, Perseus. (From the latter comes an inscribed capital of *c*.525 BCE now in the Epigraphic Museum, Athens; some Bronze Age treasures from the royal tombs at Mycenae now repose hard by in the National Archaeological Museum.) But of course hoping against hope was not enough—as the Boeotian poet Hesiod, a contemporary of the final crystallization phase of the Homeric epics around 700, could have told them.

He together with Homer was credited with laying down the basics of classical Greek conceptions of the gods' and goddesses' forms, and their functions and spheres of action, especially in his *Theogony*, a genealogy of the divine, but also in his other major poem *Works and Days*, which was mainly a farmer's almanac but carried important political and religious messages besides. In the latter poem (written in the same dactylic hexameter metre as Homer's epics) Hesiod tells a version of the myth of Pandora ('All-Gift'), the aboriginal woman and ancient Greek Eve-equivalent, created by Zeus and other gods and goddesses and sent down to earth to punish wretched humans for their presumptuousness. Out of uncontrollable curiosity (a classic flaw of women's 'nature'—as chauvinist Greek males saw it), she

21

opened a large storage jar (*pithos*), which contained both goods and evils, so that it was due to her (and by allegorical implication to the race of Women in its entirety) that the life of hapless mortal men was and eternally is plagued by evils. Only one quality was left shut firmly within the jar when she finally managed to stopper it up again, and that quality was profoundly ambiguous: Elpis—'Hope' (or 'Expectation').

The hopes of the historical Mycenaeans for a glorious future—or at least some sort of future—for their small city must have been buoyed by their inclusion on the Serpent Column: that is, the Greeks' victory-monument celebrating their somewhat united repulse of the Persian invasion of 480–479 (see further in detail the Appendix, below). But it was not to be. A disobediently independent-minded Mycenae, potentially always accessible and amenable to pressure from Sparta, was too much of a provocation for nearby powerful Argos—enemy of Sparta, neutral in the Persian Wars—to abide its continued existence. In 468 Argos simply annihilated Mycenae, causing the little *polis* to cease to be for some considerable time. (Not a unique occurrence in ancient Greece, by any means.)

When a decade later Aeschylus came to write and stage his *Oresteia* trilogy of tragic dramas (the *Agamemnon*, *Libation-Bearers*, and *Kindly Ones*), he significantly, and rather sinisterly perhaps, relocated Agamemnon's palace and abode from traditional, Homeric Mycenae to all-too historically real Argos, which just happened—or rather did not just happen—then to be in alliance with his own Athens against their mutual enemy Sparta. Herodotus stated it almost as an eternal law at the outset of his *Histories* that cities which once had been great had grown small: he could have been—and perhaps was—thinking specifically of the fate of Mycenae.

Chapter 4
Argos

Here in Argos I had the ground to be a pillow, and the world's wide fields to be a chamber...and humid vapours of cold Nocturna, to accompany the unwished-for bed of my repose.
(From William Lithgow, *Totall Discourse of the Rare Adventures and Painefull Peregrinations*, 1632)

The Late Bronze Age in Greece is also called conventionally 'Mycenaean', as we saw in the last chapter. But it might in principle have been called 'Argive', 'Achaean', or 'Danaan', since the three names that Homer does in fact apply to Greeks collectively were 'Argives', 'Achaeans', and 'Danaans'. This was at a time when 'Hellenes' had not yet come into general use as a universal descriptor; indeed, 'Hellas' originally meant just a quite small part of northern mainland Greece. Since this was central geographically and in itself politically unimportant, it was felt to be a suitable appellation for extension to the entire Hellenic world. The adjective 'Panhellenic' is first attested in the mid-seventh century, used to mean what later was called just 'Hellenic'. So the concept of a common Hellenicity—Hellenic ethnicity—spread only slowly, over several centuries, during the Dark Age and Archaic periods.

However, to call the Mycenaean Greek period 'Argive' would have risked serious confusion with the city of Argos, situated just a few kilometres almost due south of Mycenae and dominated by two hills, Larissa and Aspis ('Shield'). Whereas Mycenae lurks or skulks between two mountains and is hidden from casual view, Argos stands proud atop the steep peak of Larissa, its cone-shaped acropolis (see Glossary) effortlessly visible from the surrounding fertile plain, one of the largest and richest in all mainland Greece. (Today buried under a forest of oranges, a south-east Asian import, in antiquity the soil would have yielded chiefly grain, olives, and wine-grapes.) A few centres in mainland Greece maintained at least a continuity of habitation from the Late Bronze Age into the succeeding Early Iron Age, and emerged from the murk and gloom of the Dark Age relatively early; among the most important of these was Argos, profiting from the occlusion of both its major Bronze Age regional competitors, Mycenae and Tiryns.

The town boasts of the longest continuous occupation of any place in Greece, yet it was essentially a new proto-city of Argos that began to arise in the Dark Age of the eleventh century. This was new not just topographically or architecturally, but ethnically: a newly evolved linguistic grouping of Greeks calling themselves Dorians, traditionally thought of as immigrants from central Greece, claimed Argos as one of their three major Peloponnesian centres; the other two were Sparta and Messene. The Dorians indeed got as far south as Crete, so that historical Cnossos became a Dorian city too, perhaps actually founded from Argos, and from southern Greece they spread out east across the Aegean as far as south-western Turkey today (for example to Herodotus's Halicarnassus) and the Greek offshore islands such as Rhodes. They must have migrated east across the Aegean by sea, obviously, probably by island-hopping; but whether they also arrived in the Peloponnese by sea or rather by an overland route is another, undecidable matter. For what it is worth, later Dorian settler myth commemorated a supposed original crossing of the Corinthian gulf at its narrowest by raft from Antirhion to Rhion, implying an otherwise land-based journey from north-west and central Greece down into the north-west Peloponnese. That legend is reconcilable, using some ingenuity, with what scanty archaeological remains we have from the relevant areas in the early Dark Age (eleventh to tenth centuries).

However, archaeologically, these Dorians are in general very hard to pin down on or in the ground, so much so indeed that, in the absence of any unambiguously unique and diagnostic 'Dorian' feature of material culture, the very existence of any sort of post-Mycenaean Dorian migration, let alone invasion, has been resolutely denied. Against that scepticism, there is to be set first the evidence of dialect. Even if John Chadwick was right to detect 'Proto-Doric' dialectal forms in amongst the language of the Linear B tablets, the emergence of Doric as a full-blown dialect of historical Greek—as of Ionic (see next chapter)—is agreed to be a post-Bronze Age, early Iron Age phenomenon. The simplest explanatory hypothesis is of a population movement of proto-Doric speakers from north Greece (Thessaly?), which later, as these early Dorians settled separate, often antagonistic communities, resolved itself into variations on a common dialectal substrate, Argive as distinct from Laconian (Spartan) and so on. Herodotus, in a fascinating but inevitably wholly speculative discussion of the seven ethnic groupings inhabiting the Peloponnese of his day, has this to say of the Cynurians (who occupied a territory marginally placed between the Argive and Spartan spheres of influence):

> The Cynurians, being indigenous, seem to be the only Ionians [in the whole Peloponnese], but under the rule of the Argives they became thoroughly Dorianized with the passage of time.

Dorianization refers, apart from common dialect, to the sharing of certain institutional arrangements (three identically named pseudo-kinship 'tribes') and religious customs (an annual festival in honour of Apollo known as the Carneia). The Dorians of Argos, to differentiate themselves from Dorian Messene (Artemis) and Dorian Sparta (Athena), chose as their patron-goddess Hera, sister-wife in myth of great father Zeus himself. Her principal shrine, the Argive Heraeum (Fig. 2), lay at a distance of some 9 kilometres from the central, acropolis city-site, and it has been plausibly argued that the consciously created and maintained linkage between this extra-urban sanctuary and the central settlement on and around Larissa constituted a key to the formation of Argos's original identity as a *polis*. The most famous myth attached to the Heraeum concerns the brothers Cleobis and Biton. When the oxen due to pull their priestess mother's cart to a festival arrived too late, they substituted themselves as beasts of burden and got her to the shrine on time. She prayed to Hera to grant her sons some suitable recompense for their filial devotion, whereupon they promptly fell into an eternal sleep. Some scholars identify a pair of lifesize marble statues of young men, datable to the early sixth century BCE, as (non-veristic) images of Cleobis and Biton, but these were dedicated to Apollo at Delphi and other identifications are as or more probable. The marble used for them came from the island of Paros, which was considered the finest and purest source, and it is estimated that on average a lifesize marble figure would have taken a statuary a year to craft.

However, in the course of the eighth century even their large portion of the Argive plain was found increasingly unacceptably constricting by the expansionist Argives, and Argos came to exercise (as Herodotus correctly relates with respect to the Cynurians) a *de facto* hegemony over much of the region known as the Argolis, including the major Bronze Age centres of Mycenae and Tiryns. The establishment of this dominion sometimes involved the defeat and even expulsion of lesser neighbours, such as those of Asine on the coast, and their replacement by settlers from the metropolis; this was a form of internal colonization that obviated the need for very much in the way of overseas colonization by Argos. We may contrast the emigration that the much-poorer-in-land Corinth felt itself forced to practise in the second half of the eighth century (see Chapter 9). External influence was expressed in other, more peaceable ways too, via the

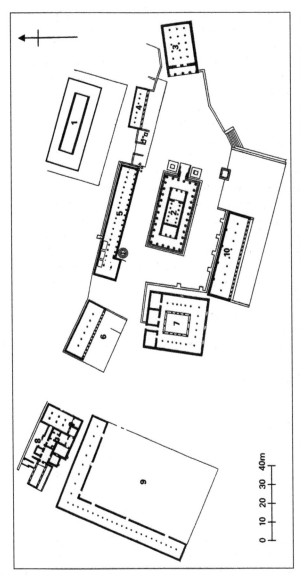

2. Argos—Argive Heraeum. Key: 1 Old temple 2 New temple 3 East building 4 North-east stoa 5 North stoa 6 North-west building 7 West building 8 Bath-house 9 Palaistra 10 South stoa

export both of artworks and of Argive-trained craftsmen. Both these are visible in quantity, especially in the shape of large numbers of dedications of bronze and terracotta figurines of animals and men, at a site destined to become one of the principal hubs of Greek ethnic interaction and the development of a common idea of Greekness: the interstate, 'international' sanctuary devoted to Zeus of Mount Olympus located somewhat remotely in the north-west Peloponnese: ancient Olympia (see further Appendix).

Early Argos was ruled by kings of some kind, mostly undistinguished apart from the shining exception of Pheidon, a hereditary king who Aristotle says rather curiously 'turned himself into a tyrant'. Unfortunately, his dates are insecure (those attributed to him in antiquity range from the eighth to the sixth centuries in our terms), but it is at least tempting to associate him with the burgeoning population and wealth of the later eighth and earlier seventh century attested by the ever-increasing and increasingly wealthy graves that have been excavated at Argos and environs and well published by Greek and French archaeologists, and with the successful military endeavours of the same period, including a major victory over Sparta at Hysiae (in Cynuria on Argos's south-eastern frontier) traditionally in 669. That marked the high-water mark of Argos's military power in historical times, and never again did Argos defeat Sparta in battle.

One of these rich 'Late Geometric' period burials, appropriately, was that of a warrior, whose family marked him out as such by including among his extensive grave-goods a fine bronze crested helmet and an even finer bronze breastplate, as well as numerous iron spits with which to roast his animal (as opposed to human ...) sacrificial victims. This assemblage also functions for us as a kind of time-capsule of the state of warfare in the most advanced parts of southern Greece in the last quarter of the eighth century. On one hand, the helmet with its high stilted crest would not have been out of place on the head of a mighty warrior as depicted in the Homeric *Iliad*, entirely appropriate for the kind of long-distance, javelin-throwing duels in which Homer likes to depict his heroes engaging. It would not have been at all appropriate, though, for the kind of close-order, mass fighting in serried ranks that—as contemporary depictions on vases and other actual finds of armour and weapons tell us—was becoming the norm in the most aggressively land-hungry cities of the day. On the other hand, the all-over bronze corselet of our Argive hero speaks worlds for both the advance of technology and the overriding concern for bodily protection and tactical defence in warfare rather than offence.

What is missing still, however, from this burial assemblage is the prime item of equipment of the new type of Greek infantry warrior, namely his shield. For it was from his *hoplon* that the *hoplitês* almost certainly acquired his title. It was known also as the 'Argive' shield, presumably because that was either where it was invented or where the first unquestionably successful and most influential version was developed. Between about 750 and 650 BCE a new mode of fighting properly styled 'hoplite' was developed that no longer depended on the heroic prowess of a mighty individual warrior, and there is some reason for suspecting that Pheidon was intimately involved with that development. But for the full implications of this new twist to the Greek story we must wait until the chapter on Sparta (Chapter 7).

Argos

Chapter 5
Miletus

> *O, Lord, yours too is Lycia and lovely Maeonia and Miletus*
> *a desirable city by the sea ...*

So begins the second part of the first *Homeric Hymn* to Apollo,
one of thirty-three lyric hymns composed mainly in the seventh
and sixth centuries BCE. The collection begins with an invocation
to Dionysus, passes through the entire pantheon of Olympian gods
presided over by Zeus, and several other non-Olympian deities
such as the nine Muses besides, and ends with a second Hymn to
Castor and Pollux, the Dioscuri, who had a special association with
Sparta, as we shall see. The prominent place allotted to Miletus in
a Hymn that manages to encompass pretty much all the Greek
world east of the Adriatic, and include both the Greeks'
equivalents of Heaven and Hell into the bargain, is an excellent
measure of the city's pre-eminence in early Greece. Not only was it
the major player in its own particular geographical region of
Hellas, called Ionia, roughly in the centre of the Aegean littoral of
western Anatolia. (Lycia lay to the south of Ionia,
Maeonia—usually explained as an alternative appellation of the
more familiar Lydia—to its immediate west, both being more
non-Greek than Greek in origin.) But, in addition, the influence of
Miletus was spread far and wide through its central role in not one
but two phases of Greek emigration and colonization. Its focal
mention in a Hymn devoted in this part of it to Apollo of Delphi

was far from purely coincidental, either: for Delphic Apollo, as opposed to the Apollo of Delos celebrated in the first part, was the god of Greek colonization—the major wave of it, that is, that began in the mid-eighth century and ran a strong course until roughly the mid-sixth, the most important single diaspora ('scattering') of Greeks before Alexander the Great's conquests in Asia and north Africa in the 330s and 320s.

The site of Miletus itself had been settled long before the eighth century. Already in the prehistoric Late Bronze Age, Minoans from Crete and even more so Mycenaean Greeks from the mainland had made a strong showing here, and there is reason to suppose that the place referred to in thirteenth-century Hittite texts as Millawanda, lying within the sphere of Ahhijawa (Achaea?), is what the historical Greeks knew as Miletus. Following the general cataclysm that affected that part of the Mediterranean in the decades on either side of 1200, it next appears centrally in a movement of Greek people from mainland Greece eastwards across the Aegean to Asia Minor during the twelfth and eleventh centuries. Historians like to call this the Ionian migration—'Ionian' because the region that became known as Ionia (Iawonia, originally) was a major destination of the emigrants, though others went far beyond, as far east as Cyprus, and also because the evolved dialect of Greek that these Greeks spoke became known as Ionic; 'migration' to distinguish it from the 'colonization' movement referred to at the end of the previous paragraph.

Actually, 'Ionian' has a third dimension and implication. Because it was these Ionic-speaking Greeks that non-Greeks such as Assyrians, Phoenicians, and Hebrews first encountered in a significant way, the standard oriental term for all Greeks became 'Ionians'—Yavan, in Hebrew, for example (and still today in Iranian). This was potentially quite a burden to bear, but the Ionians, and not least the Milesians, proved perfectly capable of doing so. Indeed it was they—both those resident along the

Anatolian coast and their congeners back in the Greek mainland (for example, the Euboean islanders)—who most fully exploited and developed their oriental inheritances: in the shape, for example, of the alphabet (borrowed and adapted from the Phoenicians of Lebanon), of mathematics (borrowed ultimately from the Babylonians of—in today's terms—southern Iraq), and of coinage (borrowed from their Lydian neighbours some time in the first half of the sixth century).

Of the twelve Greek settlements that comprised the Asiatic branch of the Ionians, Miletus at the extreme south emerged as the most prominent, with a powerful myth-history. One Neleus 'son of Codrus' was credited with being the Milesians' oecist (Founding Father), and credited too—ancient Greeks saw these things rather differently from us—with presiding over the murder of the already resident Carian males (in Homer, 'barbarian-speaking' Carians from Miletus had fought on the Trojan side) in order to seize, marry, and breed with their widows. It's murder to found a colony, as has been aptly remarked. But it is also salutary to recall that, as in most if not all the colonial sphere of Hellenism, from Phasis in modern Georgia to the east coast of Spain, all Milesians will have carried at least some non-Greek blood in their veins, at least originally. Indeed, at Miletus still in Herodotus's day, allegedly, wives refused to sit down to eat alongside their husbands, in token remembrance of their ancestresses' shaming, and even—can this really be true?—to call their husbands by name. At any rate, this does tend to put in truer perspective the symbolic claim placed by Herodotus in the mouth of 'the Athenians'—also Ionians—in 480/479, that the fact of being Greek was constituted in essential part by 'same-bloodedness'.

The attractions of the site of Miletus are not readily apparent to the modern visitor, as once-coastal Miletus is now left high and dry some 10 kilometres inland from the heavily-silted mouth of the river Meander. (The former islet of Lade a little further south, to which we shall return at the end of this chapter, has suffered a like fate.) But excavations by Turkish and German archaeologists over the years have recovered and to some extent uncovered an enormous amount, even if most of it is Hellenistic (third century BCE) or—much—later, funded, for example, by the two rival Hellenistic period dynasties of the Ptolemies and Seleucids (see Chapter 11). At least we know that the original Miletus had no fewer than four harbours, indicative of a seaborne orientation from the start.

It comes as less of a surprise therefore to learn that Miletus in its turn became the founder in some sense of a huge number of overseas settlements, even if the figure of ninety alleged in antiquity is scarcely credible. A few of the authentically certain ones were placed strategically on and around the Hellespont (Dardanelles), such as Abydus, and within the Propontis (Sea of Marmara), such as Cyzicus. These were the antechambers to the Black Sea, which the Greeks called alternatively the Axeinos Pontos ('Inhospitable Sea') or, euphemistically, the Euxeinos ('Hospitable'). And it is the Milesian settlements actually around the shores of the Black Sea—especially Sinope and Trapezus on the south shore, Olbia (Berezan) and Odessus (the original of the modern Odessa's name) on the north—that presumably represent the main thrust of Milesian ambition and interest: in the exchange of Black-Sea-produced goods and commodities, above all grain, salt-fish, and slaves, for commodities and goods that the Black Sea either could not produce (the olive will not grow on the northern shore) or produced less well (fine, painted pottery). Certainly datable archaeological evidence for permanent settlement does not antedate the later seventh century, but that does not exclude much earlier voyaging, perhaps even as early as the late eighth century. Later on, in the sixth century, Greek artefacts are found traded as much as 250 kilometres inland up the Dniepr and Bug rivers, but the Black Sea Greeks themselves were strictly coastal dwellers.

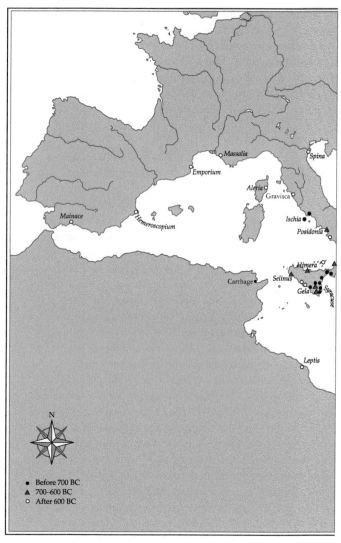

Map 3. Greek Colonization

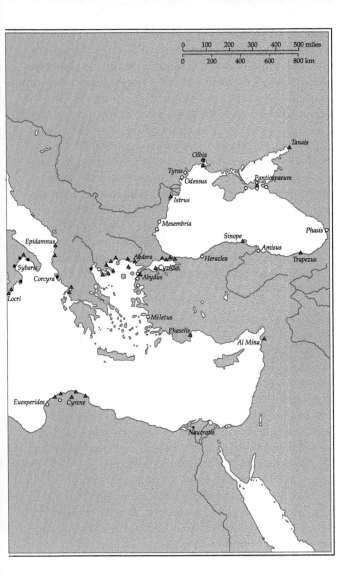

Before we get too carried away by Milesian prowess abroad it is important to remember that Byzantion, like its slightly earlier sister-foundation of Chalcedon (Kadikoy) on the opposite shore of the Bosporus, was probably founded by Megara in central mainland Greece, which had also put down a marker in eastern Sicily well before 700, in the shape of Megara Hyblaea. And closer to home the sanctuary common to all twelve cities, the Panionion ('All-Ionian'), was located within the territory not of Miletus but Priene. However, the latter fact was in itself an indirect testimony to Miletus's supreme power, since it was a constant of Greek intercity religious politics that the most important common sanctuaries were located in relatively insignificant political space—Delphi's 'amphictyony' or religious league of mainly central Greek peoples is the obvious mainland analogy, but the same principle applies too to the siting of the most Panhellenic of Panhellenic sanctuaries, Olympia, within the territory of Elis (see Appendix, below).

Moreover, early Miletus was without a doubt not only among the most prosperous of 'Archaic' Greek cities but also among the most culturally advanced and adventurous. Its cultural contacts extended as far east as Babylonia (Mesopotamia), as noted, and before the end of the seventh century as far south as the Nile Delta, where the Milesians helped found the commercial entrepôt of Naucratis and dedicated a temple to patron god Apollo. (It is probably through this commercial colony that the Western world first heard the pyramids and obelisks so named: to a Greek a 'pyramid' was a kind of bun, an 'obelisk' a little roasting-spit—soldiers' slang!) In the early sixth century it produced the Western world's first intellectual, Thales (a mini-Leonardo, who among many alleged feats legendary or genuine supposedly foretold a solar eclipse of 585). Throughout the sixth century, indeed, a whole series of brilliant pioneer thinkers emerged here—the natural philosophers Anaximander and Anaximenes, and the proto-historian Hecataeus, prominently among them; and it was here too, probably shortly before 500,

36

that Hippodamus was born, to whose name the grid-plan system of urban layout became indelibly attached. Actually, there is earlier evidence for grid-planning of cities outside the Greek sphere, but even more relevant is that Miletus itself was grid-planned before Hippodamus was born, so that the suggestion has been made that the idea was first developed in one or other of the new cities that Miletus founded before being re-exported to the mother city and then made internationally famous by Hippodamus—who, for conspicuous instance, replanned Athens's port city of Piraeus on the grid-system some time in or after the 470s.

Politics, however, were another matter. Round about 600 BCE there is evidence of a tyrant ruler at Miletus called Thrasybulus. The word 'tyrant' (Greek *turannos*) is non-Greek and probably of Lydian origin. The borrowing of the loan-word may have been prompted originally by the first Lydian ruler Gyges, who usurped power at Sardis in the early seventh century and ruled by might rather than constitutional legality. Some idea of Thrasybulus's conception of power can be gleaned from the nonverbal advice he allegedly gave to a fellow-tyrant, Periander of Corinth. Periander was actually the son of the original tyrant, Cypselus, and needed advice on how to retain rather than seize sole power, so he sent a messenger to enquire of the evidently successful Thrasybulus how to do that. Thrasybulus is said to have taken the messenger into a nearby grainfield and proceeded to lop off all the tallest stalks before dismissing the messenger to return to Periander. Further internal troubles are, however, attested by an arbitration conducted some time around 550 by leading citizens from the marble island of Paros in order to end a long-running dispute over contested land between 'the Wealthy' and the 'Handworkers'. What emerged was a compromise oligarchy shared between all the wealthiest, whatever the source of their wealth, and supported by the priestly elite.

Miletus's prosperity, intellectual fertility, and indeed very existence were abruptly terminated, by the Persians, in 494. This was by no means the first time Miletus had entered into hostilities with an Iranian power. A century earlier it had suffered from the attentions of Alyattes, fourth king of the Lydians whose capital was Sardis, inland from Ionian but heavily orientalized Ephesus. To buy good will or take out insurance cover, Alyattes had married a daughter to a high-ranking Mede from northern Iran at a time when the Medes were in the ascendancy over their southern Iranian kinsmen the Persians. But in the 550s a half-Mede, half-Persian called Cyrus (in Greek Kuros) had reversed that relationship as part of the biggest upheaval seen in the entire Near and Middle East since the rise of the Assyrian empire of the ninth and eighth centuries. Claiming descent from a Persian named (again, according to Greek orthography) Achaemenes, Cyrus founded the Achaemenid Persian empire— the largest and fastest-growing Middle Eastern empire of all antiquity.

Within little more than a decade of his first unifying Iran under his control Cyrus had extended his sway or at least reach as far as the Aegean in the west, subjugating not only Lydia (formerly under King Croesus, of the 'rich as Croesus' fabled wealth) but also the Ionian and other Asiatic Greeks in the process, and in 539 he added Babylonia (southern Iraq) to his imperial portfolio, before pushing on further north and east into central Asia. The empire was eventually organized on the basis of vice-regally ruled satrapies, at least twenty in all, and by 500 stretched from Egypt and northern mainland Greece in the west to central Asia and north-west India in the east.

Cyrus the Founder met his death fighting a central Asian people called Massagetae in 530 or 529, and was succeeded by a son, Cambyses, who soon added Egypt to the Persians' domain in 525. But Cambyses's reign ended—or was ended—abruptly some three years later, either through murder or possibly suicide; an interregnum and usurpation ensued, and many of the very recently, too rapidly subjugated peoples chose to make a bid for independence—only to be firmly suppressed, if not quite humiliated, by a distant relative of Cambyses called Darius, who made the smart move of marrying Cyrus's daughter Atossa to keep regnal power ostensibly within the (Achaemenid) lineage.

By 520 Darius had restored order throughout the massively extended Persian empire, thanks chiefly to the great guiding wisdom of the Zoroastrian super-god of light Ahura-Mazda—as he was careful proudly to proclaim in numerous texts distributed throughout his realm but most magnificently and humblingly at Bisitun, in a trilingual (Old Persian, local Elamite, and Babylonian) inscription carved in the living rock close by the road running between Persia and the old Median capital of Ecbatana (Hamadan). For the benefit of those who couldn't read any of the texts—and short of clambering up the rock-face, that meant everyone—they were accompanied by a series of massive relief sculptures depicting a Darius triumphant, under the sign (literally) of Ahura-Mazda, and receiving the humiliating surrender of a dozen rebel kings and leaders.

Not one of these, however, was Greek. For in the late 520s, whatever they may have felt about being subjects of an alien empire, Darius's Greek subjects chose to remain quiet, and out of the fray. Twenty years on, however, that choice was dramatically reversed, as Greeks all along the Aegean littoral and on Cyprus too rose up in rebellion. The revolt is usually referred to as the 'Ionian Revolt', but actually it was Aeolian and Dorian Greeks of Asia who revolted too, along with Greeks and non-Greek Phoenicians resident on Cyprus. Herodotus disapproved mightily of the revolt, as did the Delphic oracle, if perhaps only in retrospect:

> At that time, O Miletus, contriver of evil deeds,
> You shall be made for many a glorious gift and a feast:
> Then shall your wives be compelled to wash the feet of the
>   long-haired,
> And in Didyma then my shrine shall be tended by others.

Yet it took Darius six summer campaigning seasons (499–494 inclusive) finally to quell and crush the Greek rebels. The end came with a massive sea-battle off the (then) islet of Lade near Miletus. For the ringleader city, Miletus, nothing short of an exemplary punishment would do. Darius decreed that it should be literally annihilated and some of its surviving inhabitants transported to Ampe at the mouth of the Tigris. For the Athenians, fellow-Ionians, the fall of Miletus was a tragedy in more than one sense: one of the earliest known tragic poets, Phrynichus, staged a tragedy in c.493 entitled *The Capture of Miletus*, for which he was fined a huge sum in thoroughly democratic fashion for reminding the Athenians too poignantly of their sorrows.

Nor did that alone satisfy Darius. He also—in an uncharacteristic but not unparalleled show of religious vindictiveness and intolerance—ordered to be destroyed Miletus's most important shrine, that to the Ionians' patron god Apollo at Didyma, which functioned (like Apollo's Delphic shrine) above all else as a site of oracular consultation. Now Didyma was over 20 kilometres south of Miletus, but it was linked to its metropolis by a Sacred Way, much as Eleusis was linked to Athens by the most famous of such dedicated trunk-routes. From 600 BCE on, when it was patronized by an Egyptian pharaoh, Didyma had benefited from a series of costly, sometimes massive gifts, including golden objects from Lydian King Croesus, the care of which had been astutely managed by an aristocratic priestly family known as the Branchidae or descendants of Branchus. The first sanctuary on this site dates as far back as the eighth century, but in the 550s the Branchidae could afford to construct a temple in the Ionic order, mostly hypaethral (open to the sky), measuring some 85 × 38 metres, including its double surrounding colonnade of over 100 columns, each carved with thirty-six flutes. In 494 this magnificent, indeed magniloquent structure was given its surcease, at Persian hands, and the Branchidae themselves were frogmarched to Bactria (in modern Afghanistan).

Nor was it only people who received their marching-orders. As was the way of ancient Middle Eastern empires, objects too were removed as war-trophies and carried back to the Persian heartland. One particularly eloquent such trophy is a simply massive (93.7 kilograms) inscribed bronze weight in the form of an astragal (knuckle-bone) with built-in carrying handles. Pity the poor beasts of burden that had to draw the wagons bearing this dead weight as far as the acropolis of inland Susa in southern Iran, Darius's chief administrative capital, where it was eventually unearthed many centuries later.

Miletus, like another of our selected cities (Thebes, Chapter 10), quite quickly managed to re-establish itself after experiencing a total destruction. During the second half of the fifth century the renewed city came to play an important if somewhat troubled role in the history of the Athenian empire and in relations between Sparta and Athens. But probably the most famous—or notorious—native of Miletus during this period was Aspasia, although she made her name by emigrating permanently to Athens and there becoming the partner (not 'mistress') first of Pericles and then of another leading Athenian democrat, Lysicles. It was no fault of hers that she was labelled a whore and a madam, and caricatured as such by Aristophanes.

Chapter 6
Massalia

The government under which the Massaliotes live is aristocratic, and of all aristocracies theirs is the best ordered ...

(Strabo, *Geography*, 1st cent. BCE/1st cent. CE)

From 'East Greece' we move to the West, the Golden West as it came enviously to be seen by many in Old Greece, stretching from Sicily through the straits of Messina to south Italy (Magna Graecia, 'Great Greece', in Latin) and on to the south of France and the east coast of Spain. Along this route what some know as the Midi, others as the coast of Provence (from Latin *provincia*, since this was the Roman Empire's province of Gallia Narbonensis named for the chief place Narbo, today's Narbonne), seemed to the ancient Greek sailors, traders, and would-be settlers of the later seventh century BCE to be virgin land ripe for exploitation. Actually, Phoenicians from Lebanon (Tyre and Sidon principally) had passed by here hundreds of years earlier and left their mark in various ways, including—as we shall soon see—nomenclature. Other visitors included Etruscans from today's Tuscany. But for some reason neither had chosen to establish permanent settlements here, and in the case of the Phoenicians had proceeded on to Spain, to found such cities as Malaga and Cadiz,

as they founded a string of settlements on the western
Mediterranean's southern shore, chiefly Utica and Carthage,
which were in direct and regular contact with their cluster of
permanent outposts (such as Motya and Panormus, later Palermo)
at the western end of the island of Sicily.

Several cities and settlements of coastal Provence betray their
Greek origin in their very name—Antibes started out as Antipolis,
the 'city opposite', and Nice was Nikaia from the Greek goddess of
Victory (Nikê). But the greatest and most fascinating of them all,
then as now, was Marseilles, whose original name, Massalia, was
not Greek but Phoenician, meaning prosaically 'settlement'. In
about 600 BCE, just about when Thales was flourishing in Miletus,
a party of Greeks from Phocaea in that same Ionia of which
Miletus was then the most distinguished place decided to drop
anchor for good. The history of Marseilles begins with that
decision, and partly for chauvinistic reasons (it was a Massaliote,
Pytheas, among the half-dozen really great explorers of the globe,
who first put Britain on the map in about 300 BCE), and partly for
good historiographical ones, I have chosen Massalia as one of two
cities to represent the 'Western Greeks'—the other being Syracuse.

Much later literary sources tell a colourful tale of mixed marriage
involving Greeks from Phocaea (modern Foça in western Turkey)
and the local Ligurian Celts, spearheaded by the foundational
union of the oecist (founder) Protis (or Euxenus) with the
Ligurian princess Gyptis (or Petta), daughter of King Nannus.
This tale—like the foundation myth of Megara Hyblaea in Sicily,
for instance—was a myth told to exemplify the sunny, happy face
of Greek colonization, a story of fruitful and willing co-operation
between respectful Greek incomers and a receptive local
population. As opposed to the dark side, exemplified messily at
Taras (Taranto), where the Greek settlers coming originally from
Sparta in about 700 had to fight the native Iapygians for their new
home, and fight them again and again, at the cost of considerable
bloodshed and lasting resentments. But how far Massalia's

foundation myth was true—even the oecist's name was recorded variously, as noted, and the romantic element of the diplomatic dynastic marriage is surely a later embellishment—is another, unanswerable question.

Archaeology, combined with some suggestive passages of Herodotus, does, however, confirm that the founders of Massalia were indeed from Ionian Phocaea. Phocaeans, Herodotus tells us, traded in the West, not in purpose-built merchantmen, roundships driven by sailpower, but in a modified version of the then standard ship-of-the-line, the longship known as a penteconter (literally a 'fifty-oared'), powered by two parallel rows of 20–25 oarsmen-trader-warriors. Such a large size of crew reduced their profits absolutely for each completed voyage (there were far more to share them than the crew of a sailing ship); but the form of ship increased their overall profitability on average, since it afforded them some security against not only freebooting pirates but their aggressive Phoenician and Etruscan (from Tuscany) trading rivals too.

The foundation of Massalia was just one piece in a complicated jigsaw. From about 800 BCE onwards adventurous Greeks from the Aegean basin had begun sailing far and wide in the Mediterranean for various reasons: to trade, especially in metals and slaves; to obtain new land to settle, and new luxuries to import; to fight as mercenaries; or/and for the sheer fun of it. At the eastern end of the Mediterranean by way of Cyprus they encountered the Phoenicians of Lebanon, and it was from them that they learned to write again after centuries of illiteracy following the demise of Mycenaean Linear B. But, typically, the Greeks did not just borrow Phoenician letters, they created a wholly original fully phonetic alphabetic script. One of the earliest alphabetic texts was scratched in Euboean-style letters on a Rhodian vase buried in about 730 in a Greek grave on Ischia (ancient Pithecusae) in the bay of Naples. To the north-east, as we have seen in the Miletus chapter, these adventurous Greek emigrants passed through the Hellespont and Bosporus straits and settled all round the Black Sea. Westwards, as we shall explore further in this chapter and one other (Syracuse), they penetrated as far ultimately as south-east Spain via south Italy and Sicily, then either north Africa or southern France.

The hundreds of permanent settlements that emerged around the Mediterranean and Black Sea from 750 on, mostly coastal, 'like frogs around a pond' (as Plato amusingly put it), are wrongly called 'colonies'; actually, they were new independent Greek cities, or became so if they had begun as trading emporia or staging-posts. Various local, individual factors lay behind different foundations, but two goals were constant, regardless of destination—a quest for raw materials, and a search for land to settle and farm. And in almost all cases the settlers had to contend somehow with natives, whether they lived actually on the sites the Greeks wished to settle or nearby along the coast or in the immediate hinterland.

The physical attractions of Massalia, lying close to the mouth of a major river system (the Rhône) with good harbours and natural hilly defences, were immense. And the natives, if not necessarily as positively friendly as tradition had it, nevertheless did not pose a major threat to the settlement's continued, successful existence. We know little about the political system of the new *polis* of Massalia—we would have known a great deal more, had there survived to our day (it did survive to Strabo's, only 300 years later—see epigraph) Aristotle's *Constitution of the Massaliotes*, one of the 158 he and his pupils at the Lyceum compiled (see Chapter 8). But it seems to have been governed—along lines familiar from the merchant-aristocracies of medieval Italian city-states—by a small self-selecting and self-regulating council of the wealthiest citizens. In surprisingly quick time, at any rate, Massalia was so firmly established and grew to such an extent that it could establish its own daughter-foundations, such as Emporium (Ampurias) in north-eastern Spain. Again, as excavations at Torreparedones near Córdoba have suggested, what the Greeks were after were above all metals, for example those to be extracted from the mountains north of Córdoba. But the voyage of one Euthymenes to West Africa *c*.550 reported the existence of something very different: crocodiles at the mouth of what must be the Senegal river.

Many types of Greek manufactured goods passed from the Aegean Greek world through Massalia to the natives inland. Surely the most impressive single object by far was the so-called Vix Krater, a massive (1.64 m. tall, 208 kg. in weight, capacity 1,100 litres ...) wine-mixing bowl of bronze, made possibly in Sparta in about 530 BCE (Fig. 3). It was generously decorated, including a frieze of Greek heavy-armed infantrymen processing in relief around the neck, and topped off by a lid-handle in the form of a demurely draped woman. This wondrous artefact was ultimately deposited in the grave of a Celtic princess at the eponymous Vix, near the confluence of the Saône with the Seine. It represented very likely a combination of economic, social, and political investment—a diplomatic gift from the Greeks to a local native chieftain, perhaps, but at the same time a vessel with a practical function, namely to mix wine with water (or perhaps *not* mix it ... : Greeks at any rate thought it typical of uncultivated 'barbarians' to drink their wine neat) for consumption at some gi-normous Celtic carouse.

But where did the wine itself come from? Whether that mixed (or not) in the Vix Krater was locally produced or not, it *could* have been so—but only because the Greeks of Massalia had introduced the grapevine to the Provence region for the very first time just a couple of generations or so earlier. By 600 viticulture had been an established and fundamental feature of agriculture in the Greek heartlands for over a millennium and a half. Much of the wine produced there, though, was probably nothing special to taste; the addition of water, though a cultural necessity for properly civilized Greeks, doubtless also had a gustatory function. However, during

3. Massalia (Vix Krater). Excavated in the lavish grave of a Hallstatt-period (c. 500 BC) Celtic 'princess' at Vix in Burgundy, this massive 1.64 metre-high wine mixing-bowl of bronze was fashioned in a Greek workshop (in Sparta?) and transshipped as a prestige luxury item

the early historical period certain Greek winegrowing areas—most notably the islands of Chios and Thasos—had developed wines of superior quality that were marketed far and wide in terracotta transport amphoras of distinctive local shapes. In its turn

Massalia, once established as a wine-trader, created and exported, as a key element of its more general function as a major entrepôt, its own distinctive Massaliot brand of wine-transport amphora.

Some scholars would go further still and argue that it was also through the Greeks of Massalia that the growing of the olive was first introduced to the south of France. Certainly it was Ionians like the Phocaeans who traded processed olive oil to the newly established settlements of Greeks along the north shore of the Black Sea, since the olive cannot stand the frosty winters there, and their kinsmen colonists in the West would therefore have been utterly familiar with the idea of trading in oil. But even if it was they who carried the first precious olive roots, seedlings, and saplings to Massalia, these could equally and more accessibly have been grown in south Italy; indeed, there is even the possibility that it was not Greeks but Phoenicians or Etruscans (witness the wreck of an Etruscan merchant ship datable *c*.600 BCE that was 'excavated' off the island of Giglio) who had literally planted the seed of southern French oleiculture, using growths brought from their native Lebanon or Tuscany. Nevertheless, though Massalia may not have contributed much in the way of high literary or visual culture to the sum of Hellenic achievement (unlike some other Western Greek cities—Croton and Taras in south Italy, for instance), it should be granted the lion's share of the credit for disseminating to western Europe at least one liquid cultural artefact that has greatly enhanced the gaiety of many nations ever since.

In about 545 the emergent and insurgent Persian empire delivered its calling card to the Aegean coast (see previous chapter), and Herodotus tells a colourful tale of the siege by and abandonment to the Persians of the Massaliotes' metropolis Phocaea. Rather than submit to Persian 'slavery', the remaining Phocaeans followed their pioneering ancestors to the by then increasingly hellenized West. Indeed, metaphorically though by no means literally they burned their boats; that is, they cast lumps of iron into the sea and swore a terrible oath by the gods not to return to their homeland until the iron floated to the surface of the waves, i.e., in principle, never. In self-imposed exile they lived first on Corsica and then settled at Rhegium in the toe of Italy (Reggio Calabria). But, as the saying goes, never say 'never': for in much happier times two to three generations later descendants of these émigrés did indeed return, after the Graeco-Persian Wars of the 480s, and joined up as members of Athens's anti-Persian naval alliance, assessed to pay annually in 'tribute' the relatively small sum of three silver talents (see Chapter 8, below).

All the while, though, every few years at least, they might expect to meet up with their colonial relatives of Massalia, either at Olympia or, perhaps more likely still, at Delphi, where the Massaliotes had spent a good deal of their surplus wealth in conspicuous consumption and self-advertisement through the erection of a fine marble 'Treasury' to house expensive dedications of bronze vessels or figurines, gold jewellery and suchlike made by their own citizens (see further Appendix).

Chapter 7
Sparta

Night drew on apace, when I reluctantly quitted these renowned ruins, the shade of Lycurgus, the recollection of Thermopylae, and all the fictions of fable and history.

(F. de Chateaubriand, *Travels in Greece, Palestine, Egypt and Barbary*, trans. F. Shobel, 1811)

The Spartans—of all my subjects in this book—would surely have rejoiced at the notion of a very short introduction. They are the patron saints of brachylogy, the masters of the snappy repartee. It is in their honour that we still describe such an utterance as 'laconic', since one of the ancient names for them was 'Lakônes', of which *lakônikos* is the possessive adjective. Examples are legion, and legendary. One of my favourites occurs in Herodotus book 3, chapter 46, in a context of about 525 BCE. Some exiles from the island of Samos appealed to the Spartans to bring about their restoration, making 'a speech whose length matched the extent of their needs'. But the Spartans just replied that the speech was too long and complex: they had forgotten what the Samians had said at the beginning and didn't understand what they'd said after that. The Samians took the point and, when they applied again for aid, made no formal speech but pointed to an empty sack and said allegorically, 'The sack lacks barley-meal.' The Spartans' comment on this dumbshow theatre was that even 'sack' was a word too many—though they did then agree to grant the requested military aid!

For the Spartans it was deeds, not words, that counted, which is part of the explanation why our written evidence for Spartan history is so scanty—relatively, at any rate, to that available for Athens. Indeed, so averse were the Spartans to writing on principle that Sparta's laws were deliberately left unwritten, and a general ban on named tombstones was implemented, with but two exceptions: for soldiers who died in battle and—according to the preserved text of Plutarch—priestesses who died in office. (I shall return to the status of Spartan women in general below.) The exception made for heroic soldiers is telling. Uniquely among all Greeks down to the late fifth or even early fourth century BCE the Spartans actually trained for war. Indeed, they organized their whole style of life around the demands of battle-readiness, as we shall see. One reason for this unique societal orientation was their decision to enslave an entire population of Greeks, and to base their lifestyle largely upon ways of ensuring that it remained not only enslaved but productively so, providing the essence of Sparta's economic infrastructure.

That outcome was hardly predictable in the later eleventh or tenth century BCE, which is when the site of historical Sparta first shows signs of occupation after a long hiatus following some sort of cataclysm towards the end of the Late Bronze Age, round about 1200 BCE. Laconia is the name, Roman originally, that is conventionally applied to the south-east Peloponnese region centring on the fertile Eurotas valley and bounded by the mountain chains of Taygetus (2,404 m. at the peak) and Parnon (1,937 m.). No Mycenaean palace has yet been excavated in Laconia, but if there was in reality a palace to match that at Pylus in Messenia, as the Homeric *Iliad* suggests there should have been one fit for Menelaus, the brother of the great high king Agamemnon and husband to the ineffably beautiful Helen, then it will have been situated somewhere in the Eurotas valley: either towards the northern end, roughly where historical Sparta lay, or further south—recent surface finds of Linear B tablets at Ay. Vasilios offer exciting prospects.

The former location was the one favoured by the historical Spartans themselves. In around 700 BCE they consecrated a sanctuary and temple to Menelaus and Helen on a bluff overlooking the Eurotas just a few kilometres east of the town centre; and worship of Agamemnon, Menelaus's brother, is attested later at Amyclae a few kilometres south. But the Spartans' principal religious sanctuary was devoted to Athena the 'City-Holder' and located on what passed for an acropolis (a paltry affair by comparison to the Athenian, for instance); and, cultically speaking, far more important than Menelaus or Helen, or even Agamemnon, were the sanctuary of the local vegetation and fertility goddess Orthia (later assimilated to Artemis, goddess of the hunt and the wild margins and of age-transitions from sexual immaturity to maturity), right on the banks of the Eurotas, and the sanctuary devoted to Apollo and Hyacinthus that was situated to the south at Amyclae, an integral part of the city of Sparta, politically speaking.

I begin thus with religion, because although for all ancient Greeks religion and politics went hand in hand, the Spartans seem to have been quite exceptionally pious, or superstitious. Twice Herodotus says that the Spartans rated religious matters as more important than purely mortal affairs—well, all Greeks did that, so what the well-travelled historian must have meant was that for the Spartans a conception of pious duty was considered overriding in ways that were not necessarily the case for any other Greeks. Omens and portents were always taken deadly seriously by them. For example, their entire code of laws and discipline was attributed to an oracular pronouncement of Apollo of Delphi. In this they differed from many other Greek cities, who relied on Delphic Apollo rather

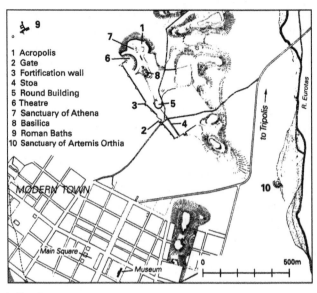

4. Sparta

for the authorization of external settlements. But this was for the very good reason that the Spartans established only the one overseas colony (Taras, modern Taranto, in south Italy), in sharp contrast to, say, Miletus with its many dozens of scattered offshoots abroad.

Mythically, the Spartans ascribed the foundation of their city to the 'descendants of Heracles' and spun a complicated tale of how these great-grandsons of the super-hero had 'returned' to the Peloponnese from exile to regain their rightful possession, along with the Dorians (on whom, see Chapter 4). In sober archaeological reality, occupation of the site of Sparta, as mentioned, is first attested in the later eleventh or early tenth century, and there is a sharp cultural gap at Sparta—unlike at Amyclae—between the latest Bronze Age and the earliest Dark Age material. Indeed, apart from some humble painted pottery and a few painted spindle-whorls found at the sanctuary of Orthia, and rather more material including some crude bronzes from the Amyclaeum, there is hardly anything to attest even habitation, let alone prosperity, before the eighth century, and the second half of the eighth century at that.

This was when, according to traditional ancient dating, the Spartans made the remarkable, and fateful, decision to expand—actually more than double—their home territory by conquering and permanently occupying that of their neighbours in what since Homeric times at least was known as Messene. In the process of occupation they also subjugated the principal portion of the local Messenian population, that which inhabited the fertile Pamisus valley (just as large and more fertile even than that of the Eurotas), and turned them into a collective body of serf-like primary producers called Helots (literally 'captives'). This conquest and occupation at a stroke solved any possible issues of land-shortage globally speaking; though it remained a contentious issue to decide how the new take was to be distributed among the Spartans. But the occupation and subjugation also ensured that the Spartans found themselves entangled forever with an enemy within: for these Messenians were Dorian Greeks, just like the Spartans themselves, and many of them managed to retain some sort of self-consciousness precisely as a once-free Greek people which had been unjustly, almost unnaturally, deprived of their Hellenic birthright of freedom. Moreover, when occasion allowed, these Helots were prepared to rise up in rebellion to reclaim that birthright. The first such occasion of revolt came in the mid-seventh century, just a couple of generations after their original conquest, and was prompted or at least encouraged by a major Spartan defeat at the hands of the Argives at Hysiae in 669 (see end of Chapter 4). It took the Spartans many years to quell this first major rebellion, and, once it had been quelled, they voluntarily imposed on themselves a kind of internal mutation or even revolution that transformed Sparta into a special kind of Greek city.

The reforms were attributed to a legendary lawgiver whom they named Lycurgus (literally, 'wolf-worker'), but he could not possibly have introduced at one fell swoop all the reforms with which he was credited, and it is not beyond the bounds of credibility that he never actually existed as a real human being. At any rate, he received religious worship in Sparta later on, as a kind of god rather than as an originally mortal hero. The three key aspects of the 'Lycurgan' reform package were economic, politico-military, and social.

Economically, some kind of land-distribution occurred, principally of the new Messenian take, such that all Spartans were given access to a certain minimum amount of land (known as a *klaros* or 'lot') together with a certain number of communally owned and enslaved Helot families to work it for them. Spartan soil, aspect, and climate in both Laconia and Messenia were (and still are—hence the famously delicious Messenian 'Kalamata' variety) peculiarly favourable to growing olives, which must be one part of the explanation for a particularly influential Spartan cultural invention: the practice by adolescent and adult males of taking athletic or other physical exercise stark naked (the Greek for 'nude', *gumnos*, is the basis of the Greek *gumnasion*, our 'gym') and then, after scrubbing down with a bronze scraper (*strigil*), anointing themselves liberally with olive oil. A special kind of container was invented to hold the oil, called *aryballos*, and both painted clay and bronze versions of them might be offered up as dedications to the gods and goddesses, for example to Athena and Artemis in Sparta. Other Greeks followed the Spartans' lead, until exercise and athletic competition for males in the nude not only imparted a specially masculine inflection to the great Panhellenic games such as the Olympics and soon after gave rise to the distinctively Greek type of statue known as the *kouros* (adolescent youth or young man) in bronze or stone, but was also used as a distinguishing cultural marker of superiority over non-Greek 'barbarians'—who Greeks liked to believe were ashamed to display their flabby bodies in public.

Politico-militarily, all Spartans became equal voting members of a primary warrior-assembly—but they voted by shouting rather than balloting, and above the Assembly remained an aristocratically inflected Senate (called Gerousia) of just thirty elder statesmen, of which the two Spartan kings (hereditary joint-sovereigns, drawn always from the same two aristocratic families) were ex officio members. The divine twins Castor and Pollux, the Dioscuri, had a special association with Sparta, since images of them were carried onto the field of battle as heavenly symbols of the earthly dyarchy. Apart from the kings, the other twenty-eight members of the Senate—elected also by the shouts of the Assembly—really were elder statesmen, since as well as being of aristocratic descent candidates had to be aged at least 60 and were elected for life. All full Spartan citizens (adult males, of correct birth and upbringing) were equipped to fight as hoplites, perhaps as many as 8,000 or 9,000 of them in the seventh and sixth centuries. In all other Greek cities only a relatively small proportion, perhaps a third or so on average, were hoplites—so if the 'modal' size of a typical Greek citizen body was between 500 and 2,000, then a typical Greek city's hoplite force would have numbered fewer than 1,000. Sparta could count on nine or ten times that number.

And on a regular basis too, since Sparta's social organization was geared towards fitting tightly and harmoniously with the military. From the age of 7 a Spartan boy would be 'educated' communally, centrally, under state-controlled supervision. The title of the new state's chief executives, the five annually elected Ephors, which literally meant 'overseers', had a special application to the boys aged from 7 to 18 undergoing the comprehensive and compulsory Spartan schooling—or drilling. The most famous Spartan to hold the post of Ephor was Chilon, who flourished in the mid-sixth century and had connections by marriage to both the Spartan royal houses. By a custom that was especially prevalent in Sparta he was officially worshipped after his death as a hero—that is, someone who had been born wholly mortal but after death was deemed to have risen above the purely mortal state and to deserve the appropriate religious cult. The same heroic cult was also accorded automatically to all Spartan kings, however successful or otherwise in their lifetime.

Spartan citizenship was a great prize; indeed, it was not a legal entitlement for all who were born to Spartan parents but had to be earned. The first test to be passed was successful passage through all the stages of the upbringing. (For an elite few, there was an extra stage of testing added on, for the years between 18 and 20, which involved the near-adults 'going wild', living off the land—and their wits—individually, away from the normal hypersupervised routines of the city, and, as a kind of proof of manhood test, killing any Helots they might encounter, under cover of darkness, although armed with just a dagger and no other offensive or defensive equipment. These 'Kryptoi', or 'secret personnel', thus injected an element of official state terror into the anyhow tense relations between Sparta and the Helots, who not surprisingly perhaps could be likened, by Aristotle, to an enemy forever lying in wait to exploit their masters' misfortunes.)

Already in the later eighth century Sparta had begun to expand its horizons as far north-east as Argos's territory and so inevitably to tangle with Argos. Most ancient Greek warfare took the form of conflicts of some sort over land between neighbours. In the first half of the sixth century, by which time the 'Lycurgan' reforms had had plenty of time to take root, the Spartans felt they should expand also due north up the Eurotas valley and into Arcadia. Here, though, they experienced an unexpected reverse in the plain of Tegea and decided to content themselves with a symbolic hegemony rather than a material occupation. But it is a clear sign of their utter confidence that neither Argives nor Arcadians nor the men of any other city were ever likely to make an assault upon them by land that they built no city-walls—until the second century BCE, in fact (although by then the city had been penetrated by a hostile force—see Chapter 10). Indeed, in a physical sense the city of Sparta remained only quasi-urbanized, and the five 'villages' of which the city was composed (the four original ones, plus Amyclae by the mid-eighth century) retained some sort of separate and individual identity. For example, the four original ones formed teams to compete in sporting contests against each other, and the men of Amyclae had a special devotion to their local god Apollo and his annual festival of the Hyacinthia, as opposed to the annual festival of the Carneia, also in honour of Apollo, but common to all Dorians.

The real-life Sparta that emerged in the eighth and seventh centuries was thus a tough warrior community, whose power and massive 8,000-square-kilometre territory (the largest by far in all Greece; Syracuse's 4,000 came a long way second) were based on exploiting as quasi-serfs the native Greeks they cruelly called Helots ('captives'), and on a strict military discipline imposed centrally on all Spartan males from a very young (though hardly tender) age. In all the 'Archaic' age of Greece (seventh and sixth centuries) Sparta was easily the single most powerful Greek state by itself. From the middle of the sixth century on, it chose to consolidate this hegemony by forming a military-political alliance based mainly on Peloponnesian cities (hence the modern name 'Peloponnesian League'). Not the least function of this was to act as a shield against potential Helot rebellion from within. It was as undisputed head of this alliance that Sparta spearheaded the unpredictably successful Greek resistance to Persia in 480–479.

Already in the 540s Sparta had been appealed to for aid by Croesus, King of Lydia, as he was being threatened by the rising Achaemenid Empire of Cyrus. But rather than involve themselves militarily on the continent of Asia the Spartans sent Cyrus a stiff diplomatic note, ordering him to keep his hands off their Lydian friend—to which Cyrus allegedly replied contemptuously, 'Who are these Spartans?'! So it was not until the long reign of the powerful Spartan king Cleomenes I (*c.*520–490) that Sparta's attitude to Persia became a matter of urgent practical politics. The rather murky end of Cleomenes's reign and life coincided with the

Persians' first invasion of mainland Greece, which culminated, disastrously for them, in the Athenian triumph at Marathon (see next chapter). But though the Spartans were agreed with the Athenians on the need to resist the Persians without qualification, the Spartan army did not actually manage to join up with the Athenians on time before that famous battle—allegedly because a prior religious duty prevented the Spartans setting off from Sparta in time, but possibly also because they were then having one of their periodic bouts of difficulties with rebellious Helots at home.

Ten years later the situation was very different. Xerxes had succeeded his father Darius as Persian Great King in 486, and once he'd sorted out his own pressing internal imperial problems in Babylonia and Egypt he turned his attention full-time from 484 on to settling the 'Greek question' once and for all. His simply massive expedition was launched by land and sea in 480, and is the main narrative subject of Herodotus's historical masterpiece. To his eternal credit, the Halicarnassian does not spare the Greeks' blushes, revealing that more Greeks actually fought on the side of the Persians than against them, and bringing to light the squabbling that went on even amongst the tiny handful of resisting Greek cities and communities—a mere thirty-one of them out of at least 700 in mainland Greece alone—even after Xerxes's troops had penetrated deep into the Greek mainland. One group, the Phocians, he said, decided to fight against the Persians only because their neighbours the Thessalians were on the Persian side! As for the men of Argos, they *de facto* 'medized' (our enemy's [Sparta's] enemy is our friend), but without going quite to the lengths or depths of active collaboration that later were to haunt Thebes's memory.

Herodotus personally chose to assign the greater share of the credit for successful resistance to Athens, which led the loyalist Greek effort by sea, winning above all the Battle of Salamis in August 480, with its superior navy funded by local silver. But at least as important was the Spartans' morale-boosting, self-sacrificing resistance at the pass of Thermopylae a few weeks earlier, and, crucially, their role in the decisive battle on land at Plataea in Boeotia in the summer of 479. The naval operation shortly after at Mycale in Asia Minor near to the island of Samos was just a mopping-up exercise.

Sparta thus—together with Athens—'won' the Graeco-Persian Wars, and so enabled the extraordinary subsequent florescence of Greek high culture that is often referred to as the Greek 'Golden Age'. But Sparta played little or no part itself in that florescence. That is a story associated essentially with the subject of our next chapter, Athens. On the other hand, Sparta's influence over not just ancient Greek history and culture but much more of the Western tradition was by no means spent. From the end of the fifth century—and as a direct effect of the politico-military and cultural antagonism between Sparta and Athens—there developed a phenomenon known to modern historians as the Spartan 'mirage' or 'myth'. Sparta came to be set up on a pedestal by both theorists and practical politicians either as a model ideal state to be imitated, as the 'Laconizers' (pro-Spartans) wished, or alternatively as a model of everything that should be excoriated and avoided.

The role and social status of women, who by conventional Greek standards seem unusually 'liberated' (they could own and dispose of landed property in their own right, for instance), the place of the Helots (see above), and attitudes to outsiders (Sparta appeared extraordinarily xenophobic)—these were just three of the most controverted and controversial areas for continuing debate or propaganda. And it was both a consequence of its iconic status and a further fillip to the myth's development that under the early Roman imperial domination Sparta turned itself into a kind of 'theme-park' of its imaginary ancient self. Plutarch, notably, who was a major contributor to the myth (he wrote a hagiographic 'biography' of Lycurgus, for example), visited Sparta in c.100 CE to watch Spartan youths being flogged to within an inch of their life (or beyond) for the entertainment of foreign tourists such as he. Perhaps it was a mercy that in the 260s a marauding band of 'barbarians' known as the Heruli devastated physically an already spiritually enervated community.

Despite these ancient vicissitudes ancient Sparta has usefully bequeathed to us English-speakers three loan-words: 'helot', used generically to mean any member of a subaltern or oppressed group or people; 'laconic' (above); and, most obviously, 'spartan'—austere, spare, self-denying. Yet anyone visiting Sparta in the seventh or sixth century BCE and seeing the usual array of Greek artefacts being produced, consumed locally, and exported—especially nicely decorated fired-clay drinking-goblets and finely crafted bronze vessels (such as the Vix Krater, Chapter 6) and figurines—would have been astounded at the socioeconomic transformation required to make Sparta as it were 'spartan', as it had certainly become by the fourth century BCE at the latest.

The likeliest explanation, in one word, is the Helots. The price for the Spartans of survival on the basis of exploiting Helot labour power was to have to turn their city into a kind of military barracks—though there was a compensation too, a huge one. From the mid-seventh century to the early fourth Sparta was easily the most powerful single Greek city in infantry warfare in the entire Hellenic world. And, in 480–479 at least, Sparta played a role in determining the future course of all Greek—and Western—history that was by no means entirely selfish or despicable. Though itself an 'archaic' city in many ways, it thereby enabled the flowering of Greek Classicism.

Chapter 8
Athens

Masterpieces are not single and solitary births; they are the outcome of many years of thinking in common, of thinking by the body of the people, so that the experience of the mass is behind the single voice.

(From Virginia Woolf, *A Room of One's Own*)

It was a dark and stormy night...'. So began a novel by the Victorian fabulist Edward Bulwer Lytton (author of the bestselling *The Last Days of Pompeii*), and so goes the annual Bulwer Lytton prize for the ghastliest opening of a contemporary work of fiction. But Lytton was a fabulist of a different sort too, as has only recently been made widely known. He was one of the very first, if not actually the first, to proclaim the virtue of ancient Athens as the forerunner, indeed founding mother, of Democracy. Thitherto the Western tradition of political thought and ideology had been overwhelmingly anti-democratic and, correspondingly, pro-Spartan. But the rise of a new, modern kind of representative democracy above all in the United States and Britain, the establishment of a new Greek state, and the increasing prestige throughout Western Europe of ancient Greece as a supposed political ancestor and role-model in the nineteenth century meant that attitudes to Athens's in fact very different, direct style of democracy softened remarkably. The enhanced esteem of Athens from the 1830s on has held its own to this day, helped by the association of Sparta with authoritarian or totalitarian regimes, and reinforced by admiration for Athens as what Plato called 'the city hall of Wisdom' and Thucydides's Pericles hailed as 'an education for all Hellas'—giving birth to an extraordinary flourishing of high culture based on notions of freedom and equality (only for some, of course).

Not only did Classical Athens, helpfully located 8 kilometres inland, grow to be the biggest city in the Greek world before the foundation and rise of Alexandria in Egypt, but it was also by far the most complex Greek city. Indeed, one could say that in a sense 'Athens' is misleadingly reductionist, for it was actually three cities rolled into one. First, there was Athens considered as a political entity, a *polis*, that is, an urban centre together with its surrounding *khôra* or countryside known as Attikê (literally, 'the land of the Athenians') encompassing some 2,400 square kilometres (1,000 square miles)—placing it at no. 3 (after Sparta and Syracuse) in the entire Greek world, and in the top 10 per cent (about 100) of *poleis* possessing above 500 square kilometres. (The 'normative' *polis* had a territory of fewer than 100.) Looked at differently, this entity was composed from about 500 BCE onwards of no fewer than 139 demes or 'villages', all but a handful of them located in the countryside as opposed to the urban centre. Second, there was the Athenian Akro-Polis, or 'High City' located within that wider entity, which was sometimes referred to simply as 'polis', a mark of its symbolic centrality (Fig. 5). This perhaps had been the location of a Mycenaean palace, and as late as the sixth century had possibly served as the seat of government for a family of 'tyrants' or autocrats, known as the Pisistratidae, or 'Pisistratus and his descendants'. But by 500 BCE at the latest it had become an overwhelmingly religious space, even if the Athenians' attitudes to religion were so different from ours that they could see nothing odd in housing the state's principal financial reserves, its 'central bank', in a temple (the Parthenon). Linked to it organically at its foot from about 600 on was the Agora, literally the place of civic gathering, the commercial as well as political heart of Athens; and nearby, within sight, was the Pnyx hill, where met the Athenian Assembly (*ecclêsia*) in the post-tyranny democratic period. Third, the *polis* (political entity) of Athens was the only Greek city to have spawned a 'double', a second city in the urban sense within its territory, viz. its port city of Piraeus; this grew to such a degree and at such a pace in the fifth century BCE that the Athenians called in Hippodamus from Miletus to try to tame and to zone its sprawl on something like a grid-pattern of streets and public spaces.

For those reasons alone Athens would surely seem to merit three times the space allotted to any other Greek city that one might choose to single out. But for various reasons, both endogenous and exogenous, Athens has also generated many more times more data, archaeological and art-historical as well as written, than any other city. As a character in a dialogue of Cicero nicely puts it, 'Wherever we go in this city, we seem to be stepping on a piece of history'. And as neat an example as any of this deeply stratified history was made known in 2002, with the excavation of a marble slab recording 80 names of Athenian citizens—casualties it is claimed of the Sicilian expedition (below). The slab, originally from a cenotaph displayed in the Classical city's chief public cemetery, the Cerameicus ('Potters' Quarter'), had been incorporated in a defensive wall of the late Roman period (fourth to fifth century) and was excavated below a Neoclassical building of the nineteenth century as part of the preparations for the display there of the Benaki Museum's Islamic collection (the eponymous Benaki being a Greek from Alexandria in Egypt).

The resulting scholarly and popular tendency towards Athenocentricity is of course rigorously to be guarded against, but it is very hard indeed to limit Athens's word-share here in line with that granted to the other chosen cities without appearing to be merely eccentric or capricious. There is a further complicating or aggravating factor: for a period from about 450 to 400, which is often labelled a 'Golden Age' or the 'Periclean' Age, after its greatest statesman, the history of the entire Greek world can and indeed should be written around the history of Athens.

Mythically, like Cnossos, Mycenae, Argos, and Sparta, and indeed any Greek city of any antiquity or pretensions, Athens was able to point to a fabled past. One of its foundation myths actually represented two Olympian deities—Athena and Poseidon—as engaging in a rather unseemly contest for the role of principal city patron or presiding genius: a contest in which Athena had perhaps an unfair advantage by virtue of her very name, not to mention her unique birth from the head of her father Zeus. Anyway, Athena triumphed, helped further by her warlike persona, her concern with practical wisdom and skills, and, not least, her useful gift to Athens of the olive-tree. On Classical Athenian silver coins the helmeted head of Athena on the obverse (front) side is adorned with an olive wreath, while on the reverse appears her familiar creature, the Little Owl symbolizing wisdom accompanied by a delicate olive spray. Another set of foundation myths spoke of an early king Erechtheus, who somehow became confused with a snaky character called Erichthonius, but both of those were ousted in historical times by two other kinds of origins myth (in which Athens was unusually rich, a reflection of the complexity of its true historical origins).

First, there was the seemingly outrageous claim that Athenians were descended ultimately from the very soil of Attikê itself, from which the aboriginal Athenians had been born. The aim and function of this myth of 'autochthony' were to reinforce an invented, artificial sense of close genetic community among a people of in fact very diverse origins and backgrounds. Second, there was the congeries of myth surrounding Athens's supposed founding 'national' hero, Theseus. Not only was he credited with bringing about the synoecism of Attica, that is, the synthesis of the disparate Attic villages into a single entity, the *polis* of 'the

Athenians' that finessed the separate identities of the various villages and districts. On top of that, when Athens had become a democracy in about 500 BCE, Theseus was credited mythically with being the founder of that political system too, although he did have to share the—no more historically authentic—limelight with the two 'Tyrant-Slayers', Harmodius and Aristogiton, who had actually killed a tyrant's brother, not the tyrant himself, and several years before democracy was in fact introduced at Athens.

Behind such myths there may lie, dimly, some correct historical memory. For instance, Theseus's slaying of the Minotaur ('Bull of Minos') in the labyrinth at Cnossos may somehow reflect relations between Athens and Minoan Crete. But the sober, authentic record of archaeology is a surer guide, and what that shows both in Athens itself and in Attica is that this region of the Mycenaean and immediately post-Mycenaean world suffered less severely than some others, for example Messenia in the south-west Peloponnese, and recovered far more quickly from the catastrophe of *c*.1200, lending some credibility to the mythic notion that Athens played some important role, if only as a marshalling centre, in the 'Ionian migration' of the eleventh and tenth centuries (see Chapter 5). Any real economic 'take-off', however, is not detectable before the mid-ninth and especially the eighth centuries, when the evidence of graves from the Cerameicus cemetery above all suggests some major improvement in both domestic prosperity and external communications; there may indeed have been substantial immigration, including that by skilled craftsmen from Phoenicia (the ultimate source of the new Greek alphabetic literacy, as we saw).

The seventh century, however, archaeologically, seems to have been a time of recession for Athens and Attikê, and when the city emerges from the relative gloom into the light of something like credible history, it is to be found in a state of *stasis*—a word that could encompass anything from civil disturbance or strife to outright civil war. Somewhere around 620 a lawgiver called Draco sponsored a series of measures prescribing drastic punishments (whence our 'draconian') for a variety of crimes. But if that was intended to quell political unrest, it failed, since a second, far more effective lawgiver was required, and it is with the career of Solon that the history proper of Athens begins. Himself a wealthy aristocrat, in 594 he was called upon *in extremis* to resolve a complicated political struggle. This was being fought out between old-style, reactionary aristocrats, the more progressive aristocrats like himself, and other rich non-aristocrats, on one side, and, on the other, the mass of the poor citizens of Athens, the *dêmos*, as Solon refers to them in his poems, many of whom were in crippling debt to one or other kind of rich citizen. This *stasis* of 594 was not the first nor by any means the last *stasis* to afflict Athens—the most notable of the series perhaps being those of 411 and 404, to which we shall return. What distinguishes this one is that Solon's solution proved so workable and enduring that in retrospect it could seem to have anticipated in crucial ways the democratic revolution of the end of the sixth century. For that formidable achievement alone Solon merited his inclusion among some lists of the 'Seven Sages' of old Greece.

Between Solon's limited empowerment of the Athenian citizen masses and Cleisthenes's far more radical, truly democratic empowerment in 508/7 (*dêmokratia* means 'power of the *dêmos*') came the dynastic tyrant regime of the aristocrat Pisistratus (died 527) and his son Hippias (overthrown 510, four years after the murder of his brother by the 'Tyrant-Slayers'). What these Pisistratids achieved above all, partly by basing themselves on Solon's economic and political reforms, was to bring about a strong sense of Athenian—or rather Attic—cultural unity and a weaker but still significant degree of participation in everyday politics by ever-widening layers of the population. Cleisthenes, therefore, the man credited with godfathering the democratic reform-package of 508/7, had a firm foundation on which to erect his new political structure, based on a redefinition of the state's political geography.

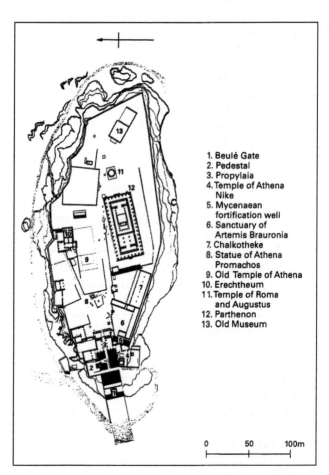

1. Beulé Gate
2. Pedestal
3. Propylaia
4. Temple of Athena Nike
5. Mycenaean fortification well
6. Sanctuary of Artemis Brauronia
7. Chalkotheke
8. Statue of Athena Promachos
9. Old Temple of Athena
10. Erechtheum
11. Temple of Roma and Augustus
12. Parthenon
13. Old Museum

0   50   100m

5. Athens—Acropolis

Besides vastly increasing the degree of popular participation, this reform also increased Athens's military potential immeasurably.

Athens's participatory potential was fulfilled magnificently on the battlefield of Marathon in eastern Attikê in the summer of 490. Athens's later military history would lead one to expect that

Athens must always have been strong chiefly on the sea, but actually it wasn't until the very decade that culminated in Marathon and the one succeeding it that Athens turned its collective mind seriously to developing naval strength. Marathon therefore was essentially a hoplite victory, masterminded by a strategist with a colourful past, a for-long émigré aristocrat called Miltiades who back in the 510s had wielded a personal tyranny in the Persian interest in the Thracian Chersonese, what we today think of as the Gallipoli peninsula to the west of the Dardanelles (Hellespont).

But after the democratic revolution of 508/7 the Athenians came to see the empire of Persia as a wicked oriental despotism, from which Athens's Ionian kinsmen of Asia Minor deserved to be liberated. Their aid to the Ionian Revolt in 499 was (as we have seen in Chapter 5) both inadequate to secure the Ionians' liberation and a fateful link in the causal chain leading to the Persian Empire's first attempt to pacify, possibly subjugate, at least some of the pesky Greeks of the mainland. In 490 Great King Darius I entrusted a naval assault to the command of Artaphrenes, a high-ranking member of the royal family, and Datis, a Mede (like the first conqueror of the Asiatic Greeks) with proven experience of naval command. All went well at first—Eretria on Euboea, another of the Greek cities that had aided the revolted Ionians, was destroyed and some of its survivors transported deep into the Iranian heartland. But then came Marathon, a stunning Persian defeat caused it seems largely by the intransigent boldness of the Athenian hoplites' charge, in which allegedly 6,400 were killed on the Persian side as against a mere 192 Athenians (whose fellow-countrymen transformed them into heroes to whom official religious worship was paid). Beside the Athenians there fought the men of just one other Greek city, little Plataea in Boeotia, whose own soil was to be the scene of a yet more decisive Greek victory over an invading Persian force eleven years later.

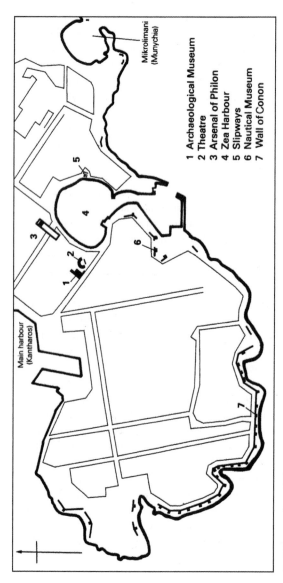

Main harbour (Kantharos)

Mikrolimani (Munychia)

1 Archaeological Museum
2 Theatre
3 Arsenal of Philon
4 Zea Harbour
5 Slipways
6 Nautical Museum
7 Wall of Conon

6. Athens—plan of Piraeus

If Miltiades was the hero of Marathon, already just a few months later he was a man of the past. The future of Athens, commercially as well as militarily, lay on the sea—as the preternaturally farsighted Themistocles anticipated. One of Athens's—and Greece's—rare natural-resource advantages was the possession of silver-bearing lead deposits in the area of Laureum in south-east Attikê; in 483/2 an unusually rich seam of this metal was struck, and rather than allow them to indulge themselves in a mass handout Themistocles persuaded the democratic assemblymen to devote the windfall to the construction of Greece's finest, largest, and most up-to-date fleet of trireme oared warships, based in Piraeus (Fig. 6). Each trireme (see Glossary) was a glorified racing-eight (170 rowers) *cum* waterborne guided missile. Light and fast, with only a very small (thirty in all) complement of officers, steersman, flute-player, and marines, the trireme was not a Greek but a Phoenician invention—one that the Greeks had been rather slow to adopt because they were not just complicated but also very expensive to build and even more expensive to maintain and crew. Only a city like Athens with abundant natural resources of silver, procured by the forced labour of thousands of chattel slaves, could have even contemplated, let alone successfully effected, the commissioning of an efficient new trireme warfleet of 200 or more ships. Not to mention putting it into highly effective action within a couple of years.

It was this fleet that destroyed the Persian (mainly Phoenician) navy in the strait off the islet of Salamis in August 480—not quite sealing the doom of the massive expedition launched earlier that year by Darius's son Xerxes, but making the task of Mardonius, the commander whom Xerxes left behind to finish the job of conquest, considerably harder. Even so, when all the odds are reckoned up, Mardonius should probably still have defeated the rather rackety coalition of a mere thirty or so squabbling Greek cities that opposed him. But the mettle and skill of the Spartans by land at Plataea in the summer of 479 were every bit the equal of the Athenians' at sea at Salamis, and there remained little to do beyond mopping up thereafter, which occurred under Athenian naval leadership at Mycale on the Asiatic coast just opposite the island of Samos. But what next? The Spartans, a landlubbing people by nature, location, and habituation, indulged their wish to withdraw from any further Aegean or Asiatic entanglements. So, the great struggle for the liberation of the Asiatic Greeks was spearheaded by the one city with the capacity and experience as well as the will: Athens.

What we call the 'Delian League' was a basically naval military alliance presided over and indeed constructed by the Athenians in the winter of 478/7. The formalities of oath-taking, including swearing solemnly by the gods that the alliance would last as long as it took not only to defeat but permanently to resist the Persian empire, were concluded on Apollo's sacred island of Delos, site of an annual festival of Ionian Greeks. The master of ceremonies was the Athenian general Aristides, nicknamed 'the Just' thanks to the perceived equity of the arrangements he imposed for regular payment of tribute and other contributions. From the start, however, it was a predominantly Athenian show—an ATO (Aegean Treaty Organization) or DPP (Delos Pact Powers), rather than an equal alliance. Most of the upwards of 200 members were small and insignificant, wholly dependent on Athenian might and good will, and mostly content to pay the required contributions in money or men as long as Athens did not unduly exploit its hegemonic position. At its height, Athens's income from both external and internal sources in the later fifth century amounted to some 1,000 talents per annum—a figure not exceeded by any Greek state until the reign of Philip of Macedon.

Within a very few years, however, some of the more powerful allies, such as the island-state of Naxos, decided that Athens was indeed being unduly exploitative and wanted out of the alliance, only to be coerced back in, with added indemnities and indignities heaped upon them. From that day to this, debate has raged over the 'popularity' of the Athenians' empire (as it is usually called)—can an empire be in any true sense democratic; or, conversely, can a democracy run an empire efficiently?

On top of the alliance's stated enemy, Persia, Athens increasingly found itself opposed—at first covertly and indirectly—by the leaders of the only other multi-state Greek military alliance with any clout: the Spartans at the head of their Peloponnesian League (another modern label). A number of niggles between the two would-be Aegean Greek 'superpowers' escalated into something like a cold war with the attempted secession from Athens's league of the wealthy and strategically important island-state of Thasos in 465. Cimon, son of Miltiades of Marathon fame, was on hand to quell this, as indeed he had been the principal architect of Athenian naval influence almost from the alliance's inception. He personally favoured a 'dual hegemony' between Athens and Sparta, and had programmatically named one of his sons 'Spartan' to make the point. But from cold war between the two blocs to hot, or at least lukewarm, war was but a short step. In 460 a conflict broke out mainly in central Greece that is usually known, oddly and anachronistically, as the First Peloponnesian War (460–445)—'First' in deference to 'the' great Atheno-Spartan Peloponnesian War that ensued (431–404).

It is hard to tell who 'won' this First Peloponnesian War. The peace agreement that concluded it involved centrally the mutual recognition by Sparta and Athens of each other's sphere of influence. Far more exciting, in terms of not just Greek but Western, indeed almost global history, are two other, closely interrelated phenomena: what was going on at Athens off the many battlefields in the decades between 460 and the outbreak of 'the' Peloponnesian War in terms of public architecture and democratic empowerment. Architecturally, the Agora of Athens began to look something like a truly urban civic centre, as Piraeus developed in parallel as Athens's port city. Up above the Agora reared as ever the Acropolis, but from 450 or so on, thanks to a massive injection of central funds masterminded by Pericles, an astonishing building programme produced above all the Parthenon (built 447–432), with its massive cult-statue and sculptural scheme fashioned by Phidias, and, later, the Erechtheum, both temples dedicated to versions of the city's patron goddess Athena.

Large numbers of outsiders, Greeks and non-Greeks, itinerants and permanent residents, were attracted to this extraordinarily, unprecedentedly prosperous and powerful imperial city. These included slave-owning arms-manufacturers such as Cephalus from Syracuse, philosophers known as Sophists (literally 'purveyors of skill or wisdom') such as Protagoras from Abdera or Gorgias from Leontini in Sicily, and craftsmen, as well as bankers and merchants and—in huge numbers, and very much against their will—slaves. In parallel Athens produced from amongst its own citizen ranks a stunning series of dramatists—Aeschylus, Sophocles, Euripides, Aristophanes . . . , historians such as Thucydides, and master-craftsmen and architects such as Phidias, Ictinus, Callicrates . . . Nor was it only Athens that contributed to the major feats of this cultural heroic age. Hippocrates from the eastern Aegean island of Cos, 'father of Western medicine', and Polyclitus of Argos, creator of a male nude statue named 'Canon' ('Ideal Standard') thanks to its ideal proportions and skilful modelling, were just two of its many other ornaments.

Bliss it was in that dawn to be alive, especially for ordinary relatively poor members of the Athenian citizen body who found their increasingly vital military role in rowing the warfleets increasingly rewarded with a significant increment of democratic political power, including public political pay for serving on juries in the People's lawcourts. The reforms of Ephialtes assisted by the young Pericles in 461 set the seal on half a century of democratic advance. Rarely indeed have ordinary people been so empowered—ordinary adult male citizen people, that is, since the Athenians were jealous of their perks and privileges, and, as the citizen body soared up to the 50,000 mark (out of a total population of some 250,000–300,000, as against the 'normative' *polis*'s few hundreds or thousands), they were quick to clamp tight restrictions on access via marriage laws; the most important of these, sponsored by none other than Pericles in 451, prescribed that to be a citizen one had to have been born not just male but the son of two lawfully wedded Athenian citizen parents.

One reason for legislating in this way was the exceptionally large number of metics or resident aliens attracted to Athens chiefly for economic reasons from other parts of the Greek world and indeed from outside it too, for example Phoenician Citium on Cyprus. Metics are attested in some seventy Greek cities, but easily the largest contingent, some 10,000 at the maximum, was to be found at Athens, despite the fact that both sexes had to pay a monthly poll tax, and the adult males were liable for conscription, besides being required to be registered in a deme via a citizen sponsor. Some Athenian metics, indeed, were sufficiently wealthy and cultivated or in other ways attractive to get to know Athenian citizens on very intimate terms indeed: one thinks again of Aspasia of Miletus, Pericles's partner in life (see Chapter 5), or of Cephalus of Syracuse, already mentioned, allegedly invited to Athens by Pericles himself, whose house in the Piraeus Plato chose as the setting for his discussion of political theory in the *Republic*. These personal connections of Pericles place his sponsorship of the 451 citizenship law in an interesting light: clearly this reform was a popular measure in both senses, rather than one that Pericles desired for his personal convenience or satisfaction. Even so, some modern historians think that an unusually increased birthrate will still have created an adult male citizen population of 60,000 in the 430s, necessitating quite extensive export of citizens to existing and new settlements abroad within the empire, and serious increase in the importation of foodstuffs, especially bread-wheat from what are the Ukraine and Crimea today.

With hindsight, it is easy to say that Athens must have been riding for a fall. That, too, was how some ancient Greeks saw the

Athens

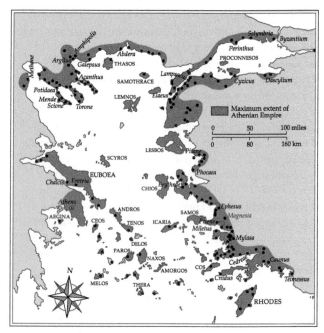

Map 4. Athenian Empire

Athenians' rollercoaster trip from *hybris* (overweening pride and insult to the dignity of other Greek cities) to *nemesis* (justified, probably divine retribution) through the imbroglio of the Atheno-Peloponnesian War, a 'world war' against the other Greek superpower, Sparta, which Sparta—with crucial Persian financial aid—won. But apart from the admittedly devastating plague that hit Athens in 430 (poignant mass burials have very recently been excavated during the construction of Athens's métró (underground railway) system), honours during the first, ten-year phase of the war were quite even, as the terms of the Peace treaty of 421, quickly followed by a separate pact between just Athens and Sparta, readily recognized.

What initially turned the tables, as Thucydides most graphically demonstrated in his unfortunately truncated history, was Athens's disastrous Sicilian expedition of 415–413 (undertaken when Athens was supposedly at peace with Sparta). The principal object of that expedition was Syracuse, the subject of our next chapter. Athens nevertheless recovered extraordinarily well from that self-imposed setback in the short run, to the extent that twice Sparta sued for peace, but on terms that Athens felt compelled to reject.

In the final phase of the War (413–404) fighting was concentrated mainly in two theatres. First, there was Attikê itself, Athens's own home territory, where a Spartan king (Agis II) occupied the town of Decelea in 413 and camped there for the next eight years, within sight of Athens's city walls. Apart from the devastating effect on Athenian morale, this occupation had three major deleterious effects: it prevented the Athenians living in the vicinity both from tilling and harvesting their fields; it deterred these and other potential investors from working the Laureum silver-mines; and it encouraged the flight of more than 20,000 slaves, most of them skilled in handicrafts, mining, or agriculture. Many of these fled to Agis's enclave at Decelea, where they unfortunately did not achieve their liberation but were sold on by the Spartans' official 'booty-sellers' to new Boeotian and particularly Theban owners (see Chapter 10).

The other main theatre was in the eastern Aegean and up into the narrows leading to the Black Sea (see Chapter 12). The warfare hereabouts is often referred to as the 'Ionian' war, since Anatolian Ionia including Miletus suffered a good deal of the action. The key players on either side were the Spartan admiral Lysander and the Athenian Alcibiades (both subjects of a *Life* by Plutarch). Alcibiades came from an aristocratic Athenian family with Spartan connections and seems never to have held any settled political views, but rather followed where his charismatic ambition and incessant self-promotion drove him. Chiefly responsible for persuading the Athenians to embark on the Sicilian adventure of 415–413, he also fatally undermined its chances of success when he was prosecuted for impiety by his democratic enemies and rather than return to face trial in Athens defected to … Sparta in 414. It was on his advice to the Spartans that the occupation of Decelea was undertaken. The combination of that occupation with hopes falsely raised by Alcibiades of Persian financial support if Athens ceased to be a democracy helped provoke a savage oligarchic counter-revolution in 411, the brains behind which seems to have been the legal expert, speechwriter, and philosopher Antiphon. Though quickly succeeded by a less extreme version of oligarchy, the regime of 'the 400' sapped Athenian morale and did lasting damage, exhibited most plainly in the Assembly's irrational decision in 406 to condemn to death collectively all the Generals in command at the—victorious—Battle of Arginusae!

Lysander was no whit less ambitious than Alcibiades and in his way as unconventional. It was through his personal relationship with the young Persian prince Cyrus that Sparta in 407 and again in 405 secured the vast influx of capital required to build fleets that could challenge and eventually defeat Athens in its own backyard. The end came at Aegospotami ('Goat's Rivers') in the Hellespont, where Lysander tricked, defeated, and destroyed a large but by then dysfunctional Athenian fleet. He followed that up with a blockade of Athens and Piraeus, until in spring 404 a starving Athens was forced to concede total victory and make an ignominious surrender to Sparta on the harshest terms.

Athens never quite recovered its old glory after 404, when, after that winter of starvation and total surrender, it suffered murderous civil war under a particularly vicious bout of rule by a junta of just thirty extreme oligarchs (the 'Thirty Tyrants') led by Critias; and, although democracy was restored in 403, Athens's democratic copybook, many feel, was indelibly blotted by the trial and condemnation of Socrates in 399. He was tried and convicted on a twofold charge of not duly acknowledging the gods the city of

Athens acknowledged (and inventing his own brand-new divinities that the city did not and would never acknowledge), and of corrupting the young, meaning that he had taught men of the stamp of Alcibiades and Critias, traitors to the democracy. The charges may have been only partially true, but a majority of the 501 jurors were persuaded to vote him guilty, and even more to sentence him to death (by a self-administered draught of hemlock). Socrates died the death of a philosopher, according at least to his most famous disciple, Plato (a relative of Critias).

Yet all the same, an age of continued moderately expressed democracy that produced a Plato (died 347), the master-sculptor Praxiteles, the orator Demosthenes (died 322), the statesman Lycurgus, and the comic poet Menander, and gave a home to Aristotle (died 322) and his Lyceum institute for advanced study, was nothing to be ashamed of. Indeed, Athens went on to recover somewhat of its old imperial power by way of its Second Athenian League founded in 378—of which its former enemy, and former Spartan ally, Thebes was temporarily a founding member. Within a decade of that, moreover, Sparta was gone as a great power. But Thebes, alas for Athens, was not, and so in the 360s Athens actually allied with Sparta—against Thebes.

The predictably fatal outcome of all this mutually antagonistic triangulation will be explored further in a later chapter (on Thebes). But, to end this chapter on a happier note, it is worth remarking that Athens, through its legacy of democratic empowerment, artistic genius, and open philosophic speculation above all, came to stand as emblematic of 'Classical' Greece in its 'best' period. As such, the city—though by then a mere village—was chosen in the 1830s as the permanent capital of the new, liberated state of 'Hellas'.

Chapter 9
Syracuse

> ... *our steps approach*
> *The rich and blessed hearth of Hieron,*
> *Who wields his rod of justice*
> *In Sicily, land of rich flocks ...*
>> (Pindar, from *First Olympian Ode*, trans.
>> G. S. Conway and R. Stoneman)

The distinguished scholar Moses Finley (died 1986) was
Professor of Ancient History at Cambridge University (1970–9).
He was also a child prodigy, taking his first degree of BA at the age
of 15—from Syracuse University in New York State. This
new-world Syracuse is just one of the hundreds of US towns and
cities, both northern and southern, named after famous ancient
cities (there is a Rome too not far away from Syracuse). The two
most widely distributed, though, are Greek: Athens (as in the
State of Georgia) and Sparta (Sparta, Tennessee, was the setting
for the famous movie of pre-civil rights racial intolerance, starring
Rod Steiger and Sidney Poitier, *In the Heat of the Night*). Syracuse,
located between Greece and Rome, can count as both Greek
and Roman.

We have mentioned (in Chapter 6) that the Western Greek
colonial world came to be seen as the 'golden' West, a space of
unusual breadth, fertility, and prosperity—in comparison to the

cramped, marginal conditions faced by the typical Greek farmer and his family in 'Old' Greece. Together with superior material conditions there went hand-in-hand alleged corporeal superiority: for example, 'the most beautiful' man in Greece at the time (round about 515 BCE) when Prince Dorieus of Sparta tried, unsuccessfully, to found a new colony in Sicily was Philippus of Croton; this city in the toe of Italy shortly afterwards destroyed utterly the fabled Sybaris, the city of luxury whence come our 'sybarite' and 'sybaritic'. But—ironic as this may seem today, in light of its more recent history of Mafia-driven mayhem, and, not unconnected, extreme poverty—the destination of choice for Western Greek emigrants from the later eighth century BCE onwards was the island of Sicily. Of all the many new Greek cities founded there it was generally conceded that it was the settlers of Syracuse who had hit the jackpot.

An origins myth had it that the nasty old river Alpheius—male as all ancient Greek rivers were taken to be—took a fancy to the gorgeous water-nymph Arethusa. Not keen to reciprocate his attentions, she fled his clutches—in a westerly direction, until she fetched up at Syracuse in the form of a perennial fountain of clear-flowing water. This myth was rationalized on the grounds that a stream of clear, non-salt water flowed all the way from the western Peloponnese to the eastern shore of Sicily. The one core element of empirical fact in the whole farrago was that a clear-water fountain did indeed flow at Syracuse, and more precisely on the small offshore islet of Ortygia ('Quail Isle'), and the hard—well, liquid—historical fact the myth was designed to 'explain' was that the first settlers of Syracuse had settled on Ortygia precisely because of the presence of the fountain they named Arethusa (which may mean 'fast flowing' etymologically). Traditional ancient Greek chronographies assigned a date of what we call 733 BCE to the foundation, and that date is confirmed, as nearly as may be, by archaeology, which has also uncovered traces of what are probably the foundations of the very first settlers' homes on Ortygia.

The founders came from old Greece, from the Peloponnese indeed, but not from where the Alpheius took his rise (Arcadia) nor from where he flowed into the sea (the region of which Elis would become the principal city). They came rather from Corinth, or, to be more precise still, from the small inland village of Tenea. One thing all descendants of emigrants to new worlds remember is exactly where their ancestors came from in the 'old country'. Corinth was the 'big city', the name of the *polis* of which Tenea was a small and insignificant constituent, and an anecdote (plausible in principle, however embellished) has even preserved what was probably the major motive behind this act of Western 'colonization'. On the boat over, one founding emigrant was so desperately hungry that he bartered away his golden prospects (in the form of a much larger and viable plot of agricultural land in eastern Sicily's grain belt) in exchange for the immediate satisfaction of a honey cake. We can only hope it was a large one and that he enjoyed it. In other words, what drove the foundation of Syracuse was poverty at home in the Corinthia, a territory of only some 90 square kilometres in all. But it was not poverty alone that did this, and it was besides a poverty bred partly of success rather than simple economic failure.

In the 730s the ruling group in the new *polis* of Corinth was a single extended aristocratic family, that of the Bacchiads, who took their name from a supposed progenitor called Bacchis. They were personally extremely wealthy, basically in agricultural land, but also because they were exploiting without stint the passing trade that used one or other of Corinth's two ports on either side of the Isthmus dividing the Peloponnese from central-mainland Greece: Lechaeum on the Corinthian Gulf, pointing westwards, and Cenchreae, on the Saronic Gulf looking east. It would have been from Lechaeum that the prospective Syracuse settlers set off, as did those traders from the Aegean area aiming at Western markets who wished to avoid the gale-blown shipwrecking terrors of Cape Malea (at the foot of the easternmost of the three southern 'prongs' of the Peloponnese).

Corinth as a whole in Homer had been given the formulaic epithet 'Wealthy', but under the Bacchiads' regime the great and increasing wealth of the city was concentrated in a very few hands. As population increased, here as elsewhere in mainland Greece in the second half of the eighth century, so (the majority of) inhabitants owning or working only small plots of land became squeezed beyond endurance. The situation was aggravated by the Greeks' practice of partible inheritance—equal inheritance, that is, among all legitimate sons (daughters, except in Sparta, tended to be awarded dowries rather than inheritances, and in media other than real estate). So, if a family had two or more sons, pressure and opportunity might combine to recommend that the younger one(s) made a new start, a new life, in the colonial West, in 'Great Hellas' (southern Italy) or Sicily. And if they did not go voluntarily, then they might have to be compelled to go, at the behest either of gods or of men—the men in Corinth's case being the Bacchiad dynasty. It was probably one of their number, Archias, who was appointed leader of the foundation and who received the posthumous recognition as a worshipped hero that was a founder's compensatory due.

The best-known example of a divinely authorized colonial foundation occurred more or less exactly a century later than the foundation of Syracuse. The island of Thera (Santorini today) allegedly experienced seven successive years of total drought—the figure is suspiciously symbolic, but even two successive years might have been sufficient. Apollo, Lord of Delphi, the recognized authority on such matters, ordered a Theran called Battus (or Aristotle) to lead a colony to Cyrene in north Africa (modern Libya). The Therans themselves, however, were far from keen to go—they were not even convinced when Apollo told them through the medium of the Pythia priestess that he knew the site, as he'd been there personally! So they settled to start with on an offshore islet, then tried to return home as meteorological conditions there had improved. But the stay-at-home Therans took a hard line and drove the recusants off, reminding them that they'd sworn a religious oath not to return to Thera ever, and that the original colonists had been selected by the powerfully objective, religiously inflected mechanism of the lottery. And in the end, stepping tremulously on African soil but finding a warm welcome from the locals who actually pointed out to them the most favourable site to settle, the settlers of what became Cyrene prospered mightily, from a combination of traditional Mediterranean agriculture, sheep- and horse-rearing and the export of wool and horses, and the cultivation and export of a medicinal plant (now extinct) called silphium. The city experienced severe internal political upheavals in the sixth century, but prospered none the less, and in the fifth century BCE the praise-poets Pindar and Bacchylides both numbered wealthy victors at the Panhellenic games from Cyrene among their clients.

If anything, Syracuse was even more of a success-story than Cyrene. It grew to be the largest, most wealthy and powerful of all the Sicilian Greek cities, commanding the second largest territory in the entire Greek world (some 4,000 square kilometres, second only to Sparta's) and the forced labour of large numbers of the local native Sicel population, whom—somewhat along Spartan lines—they reduced to a form of serfdom and called Cillyrii (or Callicyrii). The Sicels it was who gave their name to the island as a whole, but they were just one of four separate population groups occupying the island before the first Greek permanent settlers came (Euboeans from Naxus—not to be confused with the Aegean island of the same name; other Euboeans from Chalcis and Eretria had already founded Pithecusae and Cumae in the bay of Naples). Apart from the Sicels, there were the Sicans in central Sicily, and on top of them the Elymians of the south-west, in the region where Selinus became the most important Greek foundation.

And then, parallel in many ways to the Greek incomers, there were the Phoenicians of the far west, who—like their compatriots who had founded Carthage (in modern Tunisia) and settled Sardinia and eastern Spain well before any Greeks got that far—had already founded, for example, Panormus (now Palermo) and Motya (Mozia). At key periods of Sicily's Classical history it was battles between the Phoenician and the Greek settlements—the former sometimes aided and abetted by considerable forces from Carthage, and from Carthage's mother city, Tyre, and other cities of the Lebanese homeland; the latter only by relatively smaller forces of hired mercenaries—that decided the entire island's fate. One of those occurred at the Battle of (Greek) Himera in the north-west in 480 BCE, allegedly on the very same August day as the Battle of Salamis.

It is possible even that there was some co-ordination between Phoenicians, who were subjects of Xerxes's empire and the mainstay of his Mediterranean fleet, and Persians in the timing of their attacks. At any rate, from the 'patriotic' Greek side in Sicily a figure full of self-importance and admittedly considerable genuine power made representations in spring 480 to where the (few) loyalist Greeks of the old country were in conclave, at the isthmus of Corinth, trying to thrash out their response to the impending Persian invasion from the north. He offered the support of the considerable armed forces at his command, but on one condition, so it was said: that he be made joint overall commander, on equal terms, of the loyalist Greek resistance. That offer, or rather that condition, was rejected with contumely, above all by Sparta, the leader by divine election of 'the Greeks', as the resisters simply called themselves. Gelon, for such was his name, returned to his seat of Sicilian power and prepared for the coming of the Carthaginians, which he met and rebuffed with total success.

Gelon derived his name apparently from his native *polis*, the Sicilian Greek city of Gela founded by islanders from Crete and Rhodes traditionally in 688. But Gelon transformed himself into a Syracusan by adoption, since Syracuse alone could offer the necessary power base for a man of his ambition. And the very nature of his rule—and not his alone, by any means—calls into question how deeply the republican *polis* as known in mainland Greece and the Aegean had managed to sink roots into Sicilian soil. For example, within a few generations of the foundation of Selinus in the west the city was being ruled by a tyrant—a non-elected, non-responsible autocratic ruler—who has left a still visible mark on the place in the shape of the most important Temple ('C'), constructed in about 560. And Gelon too, like his patron Hippocrates before him, was a tyrant, first of Gela (after Hippocrates's death in 491), and then of Syracuse, to which he transferred half of Gela's population, while installing his brother Hieron as tyrant of Gela. To extend his reach in eastern and southern Sicily he married a daughter of Theron, tyrant ruler of Acragas, concluded an alliance with Leontini, and doubled the home territory of Syracuse by conquest and incorporation. It was probably the Phoenician-Sicilians' fear that he might extend his sway yet further, to the north and the west of the island, that prompted the invasion that culminated in the crushing defeat, for them, at Himera.

Greeks liked to place badges or emblems of their civic identity on their official coinages. The canting symbol and numismatic signifier of Himera was a cock—since Himera sounded like the Greek word for 'day'; and we can be sure that the Himerans crowed long and loud over their defeated adversaries of 480. But Himera's coinage paled, both in weight (that is, value) and in beauty of execution, beside that of Syracuse, unsurprisingly. In an act of spectacularly effulgent self-advertisement the city issued a series of silver decadrachms, ten-drachma pieces, at a time when a single drachma would have comfortably kept alive a family of four for several days. On the obverse appears characteristically the head of the nymph Arethusa, surrounded by darting dolphins. The most spectacular of all are dated around 470 BCE, by which time Gelon had died (478) and his younger brother Hieron had taken over ('succeeded' would give the wrong impression) from him at Syracuse.

Like his brother, Hieron extended his reach through a dynastic marriage-alliance, but his ambitions extended beyond Sicily to south Italy, since he wed the daughter of the tyrant-ruler of Rhegium, just across the straits of Messina—a man claiming kinship with the Messenians of the Peloponnese who languished under Sparta's iron heel as Helots. Indeed, in 474 Hieron took on the Etruscans in a sea-battle off Greek Cumae in the bay of Naples—and won: as token of his Hellenism and as a war-trophy, he dedicated a captured Etruscan bronze helmet to Zeus at Olympia—one up on Miltiades of Marathon, who had dedicated there his own, suitably inscribed bronze helmet. A brother of his, Polyzalus, tyrant of Gela, about the same time offered up a magnificent bronze sculpture-group to Apollo of Delphi, in thank-offering for a victory in the most prestigious and costly four-horse chariot-race at the Pythian Games (478 or 474).

Like Gelon, too, Hieron played fast and loose during the twelve years of his rule (478–466) with the Greek city-populations within his ambit. He destroyed Naxus, the oldest Greek settlement of Sicily, and Catane too; their surviving inhabitants he 'resettled' in Leontini. Having first annihilated Catane, however, in a seeming act of restitution or perhaps just because he wanted to be worshipped after his death as a founder-hero, he then resurrected it in 474—under a new name: Aetna, in tribute to the eponymous volcano that had erupted significantly only a year or so earlier. He persuaded Pindar to write a celebratory ode, and, less predictably, specially commissioned a new play by Aeschylus, his *Women of Aetna*. Yet far more striking (pun intended) even than those was the unique silver tetradrachm (four-drachma) coin he caused to be produced in about 470 (now in the Royal Library of Belgium, Brussels).

The identification is given on the obverse by the eight letters spelling out 'Aitnaiôn'—'of the citizens of Aetna'—distributed on either side of a bushy-bearded, ivy-crowned Silenus (elderly satyr, part-man, part-beast, all wine-fuelled sexual lust), below whose neck nestles a peculiarly large and local type of dung-beetle. On the reverse is shown a Zeus of Mount Etna, seated in majesty on an elaborately carved throne draped with a panther's skin, his right arm resting on a vine-staff, his left sinisterly grasping his trademark thunderbolt. In front of him rises a tree, probably of the sole native species of fir, atop which perches an eagle—the king of the birds of the air, symbolizing the King of Gods and Men. Hieron, styling himself Hieron of Aetna, also sent an inscribed Greek-made helmet to Olympia, presumably also booty but this one taken from Greek opponents; it went as a dedication to the other, far more famous and long-established mountain Zeus, of Mount Olympus. Hieron's Panhellenic superstar-status must have seemed untouchable to him, but that was not how it seemed to his rivals in Acragas and elsewhere, and it did not outlast his death in 466. For when he died, something really rather extraordinary happened: what Moses Finley in his history of ancient Sicily nicely labelled a 'democratic interlude'.

The roots of democracy in Sicily are difficult if not impossible to locate in Sicily itself. Whereas democracy was Athens's own native invention, at Syracuse it was surely a foreign import—and presumably from Athens (where Themistocles, a keen personal exporter of democracy to Argos, had already been showing a keen interest in the West long before his death in the 460s). But, oddly quickly, the alien-born graft seems to have taken, both institutionally and culturally. A local form of popular comic drama associated with Epicharmus flourished at Syracuse, as at Athens, and it was two Syracusans, Tisias and Corax, who were credited with some sort of formalization of the rules of public rhetoric—the type of communication that was fundamental to the successful working of a direct, face-to-face, Greek-style democracy. Probably not coincidentally, it was another Sicilian Greek, Gorgias from Leontini, who in 427 introduced Athenians to the full blooms of rhetorical florescence.

Elsewhere in Sicily too there are signs of great prosperity in the middle decades of the fifth century—the mute testimony of a huge number of massive temples at Acragas, or the recently raised remains of a sewn-planked merchantman bearing a precious cargo of Athenian and Peloponnesian amphorae, drinking-cups, oil lamps, and woven baskets towards Gela, are impressive enough. And that was on top of Sicily's own natural resources of grain—for example, Gela, where Aeschylus died in 456, bears the epithet 'wheat-bearing' in the great tragedian's moving epitaph. So it came about that imperial democratic Athens, charged with feeding an ever-growing population with ever-increasing amounts of imported grain, began to cast its eyes longingly westwards, to south Italy and Sicily, with an eye both to Western grain imports and to Western timber for shipbuilding. Treaties, the texts of which have survived on stone, were sworn between the Athenians and the 'Ionian' Greeks of Rhegium and east Sicilian Leontini, but also, more curiously, with the non-Greek Elymians of Segesta in the far south-west of the island. And, among the precipitating causes of a conflict between Athens and Sparta ('the Peloponnesian War') that initially affected only the Greek mainland and Aegean, Thucydides placed first the dispute which broke out in the later 430s between Corinth and the Corinthians' own foundation of Corcyra (Corfu), over Epidamnus (Durazzo/Durrës in modern Albania). This conflict in turn drew Athens in on Corcyra's side, precisely because Corcyra lay on the lucrative Western route, but also because it possessed Greece's second largest trireme warfleet and, last and least, was a democracy.

During the first, ten-year phase of the Peloponnesian War, Athens made a quite serious attempt at establishing a firm presence in Sicily, but this backfired to such an extent that it produced the virtually unthinkable—a show of political unity among the Sicilian Greeks, demonstrated by a congress at Gela that was dominated by a politician from democratic Syracuse. Almost ten years later, in a period of 'phoney' peace with Sparta, Athens reawakened its interest in Sicily, and especially in taking Syracuse down if not out. This was partly for reasonably sound strategic reasons: increased availability of Sicilian resources might well be decisive in any renewed conflict with Sparta. But alongside these, there were flying around crazy notions of extending imperial domination to all Sicily, and possibly even from there to Carthage... Small wonder that Aristophanes satirized this castle-building in the air in his comedy *Birds* of 414.

Thucydides took almost the opposite, tragic tack. He emphasized Athens's hybristic ignorance of conditions in Sicily, and not least in Syracuse itself, a city comparable in size, wealth, and population and, what's more, like Athens a democracy, so unsusceptible to any Athenian charm offensive promising to the masses democratic liberation from an oppressive oligarchy—or tyranny. Within eighteen months all Athens's highest hopes had been shattered, the end militarily coming in a huge naval battle in Syracuse's great harbour. Out of so many, Thucydides epigrammatically put it, so few returned to Athens. Many indeed languished and died in the fossil-ridden limestone quarries of Syracuse, as miserable prisoners of war unaided by any Geneva Convention. The story went that some Athenians made a lucky escape because they could recite from memory the latest choruses of Euripides to their tragedy-mad captors, but those who knew only Aristophanes were presumably less fortunate.

Politically, Syracuse and Athens at first went opposite ways—Syracuse becoming more radically democratic, Athens undergoing two bouts of oligarchic reaction, coupled fatally with final defeat by Sparta in 404. But Athens was not Syracuse's only foreign opponent to contend with in these last decades of the fifth century. Very much not. In 409, the Carthaginians tried again, in order to redress their failure of 480. At Athens, from 413 on, the question had been asked—can a democracy run an empire and win a major war? The eventual answer, in 404, was a resounding negative. At Syracuse, even before an external military defeat had been inflicted, a major political defeat was suffered by the pro-democratic forces, and in 405 the democratic interlude came abruptly to an end as the Carthaginian threat intensified.

Syracuse and all Greek Sicily, it was argued, needed a single strong man, a generalissimo who could knock the Greeks' heads together and mould them into a coherent force of resistance. Unlike the resistance of 480 to the Persians, this was not to be danced to the tune of 'Battlecry of Freedom'. Cold pragmatism was the order of the day, and the man who emerged as the General Washington of the Sicilian Greeks of the late fifth century BCE was one Dionysius, posthumously Dionysius I, since he managed to set up some sort of monarchical succession based on birth. In short, Syracuse and Sicily had reverted to tyranny, and the tyranny of Dionysius was sufficiently long (405–367) and sufficiently successful (he not only beat off the Carthaginians but established a kind of mini-empire on the Adriatic coast of Italy) that it became a sort of archetype of what Tyranny in essence was: an autocracy based on military force supplied by a personal bodyguard and mercenaries; and reinforced by multiple dynastic marriages, the unscrupulous transfer of populations, and the enfranchisement of foreigners. There was a downside, however: constant terror of plots against his life. *Sic transit gloria democratica.*

The tyrant dynasty of Syracuse did not long outlive Dionysius I; there was even a democratic revival of sorts in the mid-century, including a forcible redistribution of land and houses in favour of the poor. But the future of the Greek world was to lie in the hands, not of republican regimes, whether democratic or oligarchic, but of political strong men whom the Greeks called 'dynasts'. In the wake of Dionysius of Syracuse followed the non-Greek but strongly hellenized dynast Mausolus of Caria in south-west Asia Minor: a vassal of Persia, he moved his capital from the interior to Greek Halicarnassus on the coast and was buried there in 353/2 in the aboriginal and eponymous Mausoleum, a fabulously ornate tomb commissioned by his sister-wife Artemisia and decorated by the very best Greek sculptors of the day, including Scopas from the Aegean marble island of Paros. But even this magnificence paled by comparison with that of the greatest dynast of them all to date, Philip of Macedon, under whose sway by the 330s all mainland Greece had fallen.

To enshrine and perpetuate his rule of Greece, Philip founded in 338/7 the League of Corinth (see Chapter 11). Shortly thereafter, a citizen of that latter city, Timoleon, was dispatched to help its daughter-city Syracuse out of the terrible economic and political mess it had got itself into. This was a neat reminder of how the close sentimental tie that normally subsisted between a metropolis and its 'colony' might be translated into effective reciprocal political action. Indeed, such was Timoleon's success there, and elsewhere in Greek Sicily, that he became in effect Syracuse's second Founder, and was buried in the Agora of Syracuse in the mid-330s as if he really were.

Chapter 10
Thebes

> *This has come from my counsel*:
> *Sparta has cut the hair of her glory*:
> *Messene takes her children in*:
> *a wreath of the spears of Thebe*
> *has crowned Megalopolis*:
> *Greece is free.*
>
> > (Epitaph of Epaminondas, d. 362, as
> > preserved by Pausanias, *Description
> > of Greece*, trans. P. Levi)

The chief beneficiary of the mutual attrition of the Athenians and the Spartans was Sparta's central Greek ally, Thebes. Here is another city with a foothold deep in mythic territory. It was the birthplace of the god Dionysus and of the überhero-turned-god Heracles, and (though his failure to realize it at first was to prove tragically fatal for him) of King Oedipus. It was also the target residence of choice for famous immigrant Cadmus from Phoenicia, who was credited anachronistically with bringing with him from Tyre the art of alphabetic writing; the Greeks with rather surprising humility referred to their alphabet as either 'Phoenician' or 'Cadmean' letters. Were the modern town of Thebes not plonked directly on top of the ancient prehistoric and historic cities, we would know an awful lot more about the prehistoric city built upon the Cadmea acropolis, with its

Mycenaean palace that has yielded the most recent sizeable haul of Linear B texts—including use of a word that looks something like 'Lacedaemon', the name of the region of the south-east Peloponnese that Sparta came to dominate.

Historical Thebes too had its major points of cultural interest, notwithstanding the fact that their snooty neighbours in Athens liked to sneer at the Thebans as mere 'Boeotian swine'. For in the late sixth century Thebes produced the leading lyric poet Pindar (c.518–446)—not to mention that Hesiod (flourished c.700) had also been a Boeotian, from the village of Ascra within the city of Thespiae. Thebes, moreover, developed and controlled a flourishing federal state, which offered an original and alternative mode of political organization to the single *polis*. For some decades in the fourth century BCE Thebes was actually the single most powerful city in mainland Greece and a forcing-house of the political transformation that eventuated through the reigns of the Macedonian kings Philip II and his son Alexander the Great.

Some sort of Boeotia-wide federation was in existence before the last quarter of the sixth century. A common silver coinage bearing the obverse device of an infantryman's shield attests a form of political unity, since coinage in Greece was always as much a political as an economic manifestation. This unity was expressed and reinforced in the characteristic Greek way, by a common religious cult: the Pamboeotia ('All-Boeotia Festival') celebrated annually at Onchestus. Another major Boeotian sanctuary that flourished in the sixth century was the Ptoion, not far from Thebes, which was dedicated to Apollo. As many as a hundred lifesize marble statues of the *kouros* (naked youth) type were dedicated here, a sure index of great local wealth as well as piety.

Boeotian unity, however, let alone unification, was never complete. Far from it. Indeed, such was the intestine strife among the cities of Boeotia that Pericles—admittedly not a disinterested witness—likened the Boeotians to tall trees, whose tops crash together in a storm and act as their own executioners. Within the federation a constant struggle was waged between the two major cities, Thebes and Orchomenus (another place with a major Mycenaean past), each dominating its own region, that culminated in the outright destruction of the latter by Thebes in 364. Two Boeotian cities (Eleutherae and Plataea) actually 'got away', in the sense that they became allied to, or even incorporated politically within the territory of, Thebes's main neighbour—and usually enemy—Athens. (Although the proverb an 'Attic (Athenian) neighbour', meaning a dreadful one, was not in fact spawned by Thebes's relations with Athens, it could well have been.) But the normal fate of the majority of Boeotian cities, which were small, was to be subordinated to the nearest larger entity, supposedly for the greater collective good.

As in the case of Argos, only more so, the Persian invasion of 480 seriously compromised Thebes's claims to Hellenicity. Whereas Argos feebly stayed neutral, the ruling hierarchy of Thebes actually opted for the Persian side—a sufficiently blatant and memorable act of treachery ('medism') to constitute a plausible justification, even a century and a half later, for the total destruction of Thebes in its turn, at the behest of Alexander the Great in 335. A later generation of Thebans had sought to explain it away on the grounds that Thebes was not then ruled in a properly constitutional way but had fallen into the hands of an extreme oligarchic junta, a *dunasteia* or collective tyranny. Whether that was true as a matter of fact, it reflected Greek political thought's careful attention to nice distinctions of kind and degree—though it did nothing to stay Alexander's hand.

The year 335 was the endpoint of Thebes's most brilliant four decades, the origins of which may be traced back to the mid-fifth century. Having recovered first from the humiliation of medism in 480 and then from the humiliation of occupation by Athens between 457 and 447, the Thebans re-established a Boeotian federal state on new lines, with their own city clearly in the driving seat from the start, that flourished down to 386. We happen to have an account of this remarkable federal constitution, preserved on a papyrus from Oxyrhynchus in the Fayum in Egypt, composed by an unusually well-informed and accurate (but anonymous) historian. It was oligarchic but moderately so; high office and effective political and military power were confined to the top 30 per cent or so wealthier citizens who could afford to equip themselves as cavalrymen or at least as hoplites. Citizenship of any sort was denied to traders and craftsmen, since such people were deemed to have soiled their souls as well as their hands by engaging in economic production and exchange other than agricultural. A complicated system of local representation on the governing federal Council gave disproportionate power and influence to Thebes from the start.

This position Thebes was able further to enhance and exploit as a loyal ally of Sparta in the Peloponnesian War. That loyalty was demonstrated especially in 421 when two other allies, Corinth and Elis, defected, but Thebes remained steadfast precisely because it considered Sparta's general support for oligarchy to be in its own best interests. In 427, moreover, the Thebans achieved a long-cherished aim, with direct and powerful Spartan encouragement. If they could not persuade the Plataeans, who were ethnic Boeotians, to abandon their alliance with Athens (concluded as long ago as 519, and lying behind the remarkable co-operation between those two cities at Marathon in 490), then they must at least destroy it. This achieved, a few years later they seriously reduced the independence of Athens-leaning Thespiae by tearing down its walls. During the final phase of the Peloponnesian War (413–404) it was Thebans who benefited the most economically, whether from pilfering Athenian country houses under the protection of a Spartan garrison located near the Boeotian border, or by buying up cheap the thousands of slave runaways from the Athenians' silver-mines.

But there was always a counter-current, if not quite an opposition, to the dominant political strata. At Thermopylae in 480 a number of Theban volunteers, Greek patriots presumably, had fought on the same side as Leonidas. During the Athenian occupation of 457–447 there was a strong pro-Athenian democratic faction in a number of cities, such as Thespiae. And at and after the end of the Peloponnesian War, even oligarchic Thebes grew increasingly disaffected with Spartan high-handedness, to the extent that in 403 it offered shelter to democratic exiles from the Spartan imposed and backed Thirty Tyrants junta and in 395 joined an anti-Spartan Quadruple alliance that included likewise disaffected Corinth as well as resolutely anti-Spartan Argos and, naturally, Athens.

Yet the Spartans, with the renewed financial backing of their opportunistically embraced Persian sponsors, won that Corinthian War (395–386), and exploited their victory in an extreme fashion; the peculiar animus of King Agesilaus II towards Thebes is apparent. The Boeotian federal state was disaggregated altogether, reduced back to its constituent cities and even villages, and then, to guarantee the new, reactionary order, the Spartans imposed garrisons on a number of key Boeotian cities including of course Thebes (the garrison occupied Thebes's acropolis, the Cadmea), even though that was in flagrant breach of the autonomy clause of the King's Peace (see Glossary). A number of influential Thebans escaped into exile, to Athens above all—the Athenians hereby repaying the Thebans' favour of 403.

And in 379/8, with crucial Athenian help, a band of these Theban exiles not only liberated Thebes from Sparta but straightaway placed it on an entirely new footing by introducing a democratic constitution at home and then re-founding the Boeotian federal state on the same moderately democratic basis. In this, they were for once marching with the times. For the first half of the fourth century BCE was the great age of democracy in the Greek world as a whole, not—as might have been supposed—the second half of the fifth, when democratic Athens and its empire had ruled supreme. Further confirmation of this more widespread democratic emergence in the earlier fourth century has very recently emerged from the city of Argos, where a few years ago a cache of over 130 inscribed bronze tablets was uncovered, the dated financial records of the democracy that then prevailed. However, a peculiarly vicious bout of civil war at Argos in the late 370s, known graphically as the 'Clubbing' (in a far from convivial, entertainment sense—some 1,000–1,500 oligarchs were clubbed to death), reminds us of the tenseness and fragility of political governance in these hothouse and all too face-to-face communities.

Nor were the Thebans' innovations confined to the political sphere by any means. The Boeotian military too flourished as never before, thanks both to its federalist character and to its innovative structure (a remarkable feature of which was the Theban Sacred Band, an elite strike force composed of 150 homosexual couples). All that was complete anathema to Sparta—including the Sacred Band: for though the Spartans had made homosexual relations between an adult male and an adolescent boy an integral part of their educational system, they had not also sought to integrate it into their army arrangements. Fittingly, therefore, it was Thebes under Epaminondas and his sidekick Pelopidas (one of the former exiles at Athens), together with the Sacred Band's founder Gorgidas, that put an end to Sparta as a great power for good, first by winning hands down the Battle of Leuctra in 371 and then, not least, by liberating at last the greater number of Sparta's Helots. Both Plato and Aristotle had criticized Sparta's Helot-management on purely utilitarian, pragmatic grounds. 'God has made no man a slave', wrote another contemporary intellectual in support of Helot liberation—which was as close to abolitionist talk as a fourth-century Greek was likely to get. But it took a star like Epaminondas to translate pious talk into concrete deeds.

Thanks largely to the brilliant and enlightened statesmanship and generalship of him and Pelopidas, Thebes briefly became the most important and powerful city in all mainland Greece. Not only was Sparta cut down to (a much reduced) size, but two new Greek cities, Messene (369) and Megalopolis in Arcadia (368), were founded under Epaminondas's direct supervision to ensure that it remained impotent for the foreseeable future. It comes as no surprise that Argos vigorously assisted in the foundation of Messene, and made a huge song and dance about it at Delphi. Within Boeotia itself Thebes seized the opportunity in 364 to destroy Orchomenus, its only serious rival for local federal hegemony. More surprising was that the Boeotians for the first time ever got together a fleet and Epaminondas cruised with it in the northern Aegean and even up as far as the Bosporus, but to no serious practical effect. It was further symptomatic of Thebes's hegemonic reach—not the same as grasp—after Leuctra that between 368 and 365 Prince Philip of Macedon was held hostage for his kingdom's good behaviour under house-arrest in Thebes.

Such were the temporary power and influence of Thebes in the 360s that democratic Athens and oligarchic Sparta even felt obliged to ally with each other once more to meet this mutual Theban threat, but to no military avail. For once again, on the battlefield of Mantinea in Arcadia in 362, the Theban alliance led brilliantly by Epaminondas won the day—though the great general himself lost his life (see epigraph for his obituary notice). Thereafter, according to the conservative Athenian historian and thinker Xenophon, who concluded his *Greek History* on this sombre note, there was even greater confusion internationally in Greece than before. But Xenophon's word should not be taken on trust. He despised Epaminondas's Thebes and as a loyal client and partisan of Agesilaus was one of those who yearned for the good old Spartan-dominated oligarchic order. That could never be reinstated, as the career of Philip of Macedon was soon cruelly to demonstrate.

7. **Thebes (Lion of Chaeronea). In this handsome stone grave-memorial, reconstructed from many fragments, the lion's majesty fittingly commemorates the outstanding bravery of the Thebans who died vainly resisting Philip II of Macedon at Chaeronea, 338 BCE**

The future King Philip II's three-year captivity in Thebes taught him a lot that he needed to know about diplomatic, fiscal, and military affairs when he became king of Macedon in 359. Macedon thitherto had been an outlier of mainstream Greek culture both geographically and politically. Indeed, down to Philip's reign it had for long stretches been little more than a geographical expression, being politically neither advanced (it was resolutely non-*polis* and non-urban) nor unified (the upland West was almost a separate entity from the lowland East region). During Philip's relatively long (by Macedonian standards) reign (359–336) Macedon first was unified, then began to urbanize and finally not only achieved control of all mainland Greece to its south, defeating the coalition of Athens and Thebes in 338 at the Battle of Chaeronea in Boeotia (Fig. 7) and neutralizing Sparta along the way, but also embarked on the conquest of Asia too (see further next chapter). This was the death-knell of the traditional *polis* as a power-unit in Greek history, though there are occasional later exceptions, such as the island-city of Rhodes in the third and even the early second century.

Indeed, in the post-Alexander Hellenistic period even Macedonia became a region of Greek cities, with all the usual amenities and accoutrements of urbanism, including demarcated public central spaces, spacious gymnasia, and the erection of inscribed public documents. The way had been prepared, little though the Macedonians themselves could have guessed it, for expansionist imperial Rome to make of Macedonia its first eastern province (in 147)—unless largely Hellenic Sicily (made a province in 241) is counted as 'eastern'. Following Alexander's destruction of it in 335, Thebes had been rebuilt from 316 BCE on, but on a much smaller scale, and, though a comfortable enough place to live in under the Roman dispensation, it never recovered anything like its Classical-era political and military significance.

Chapter 11
Alexandria

bird-cage of the Muses ...

(Timon of Phlius, 3rd cent. BCE)

Philip's son and successor Alexander III, later known as 'the
Great', came to the throne of Macedon in highly dubious
circumstances; indeed, a shadow of suspicion hangs over him to
this day. But his complicity in his father's assassination in 336 at
Aegae, Macedon's ceremonial capital and royal burial-ground, can
never be proved, and there is at least as much reason to suspect
the hand behind the scenes of his dynamic mother, Olympias. She
had recently been downgraded as Number 1 Queen (Philip, like
the Sicilian tyrants, broke the universal Greek rule of strict
monogamy, as Alexander was also to do), and Philip's latest
(seventh) Queen was a high-born Macedonian with vital political
connections who had recently given birth to a son. Philip himself
was a pretty hale 46 years of age. There was a severe danger that
Alexander would be passed over for the succession. Hence,
arguably, the assassination—carried out in full view as Philip was
celebrating the wedding of his daughter with Olympias to
Olympias's own brother.

But that is only a plausible scenario. Whoever was behind the
murder, there is no doubt but that it was Alexander who profited

most from it. Winning the support, crucially, of the army, Alexander was quick to assume his father's role as champion of Hellenism against the Persian empire. Philip in 338 had defeated a Greek coalition led by Athens and Thebes and established immediately after what moderns call the 'League of Corinth' as the vehicle to express and legitimate his *de facto* suzerainty over mainland Greece. The first decision taken by the League delegates in congress at Corinth was to appoint Philip commander-in-chief of a campaign against the Persian empire. The campaign was dressed up as a long-delayed act of revenge on the Persians for their sacrilegious destruction of sacred sites and property in 480–479, and as a project of liberation (echoing propaganda used by Athens from 478 and Sparta from 400) of the Asiatic Greek cities from barbarian 'slavery' (political subjection). An advance force was sent across the Hellespont to north-west Asia Minor in 336, but Philip's death necessitated a delay in Alexander's assuming the command in person, not least because he had to deal with troublesome revolts among his Greek 'allies' and to secure his rear as far north as the Danube. Again, following the example of his father, who had annihilated the important northern Greek city of Olynthus in 348, Alexander in 335 annihilated Thebes for daring to question the legitimacy of his oriental project and rise up in revolt. All he spared of the city, apart from the religious sanctuaries, was the house Pindar the praise-poet (died 446) had lived in, since Pindar was seen as an emblematic spokesman for the sort of cultural Panhellenism Alexander was claiming to promote. All the same, destroying the city of one of your most important supposed Greek allies was hardly an auspicious omen for the coming Asiatic campaign.

And controversy attended it throughout, as Alexander showed preternatural gifts for leadership and command in the most demanding of physical and moral conditions over more than a decade (334–323). Whatever exactly Philip had originally intended to achieve, Alexander surely exceeded those intentions by a very long way. He extended Macedon's dominion as far east as

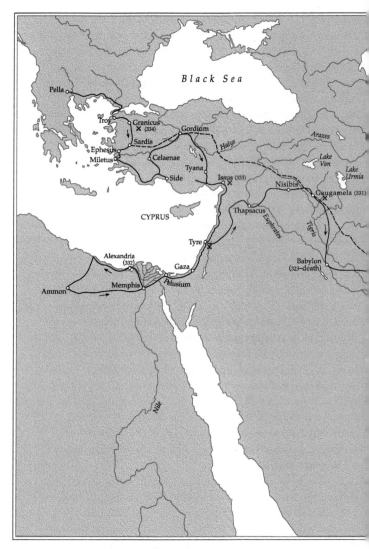

Map 5. Alexander's Battles and Journeys

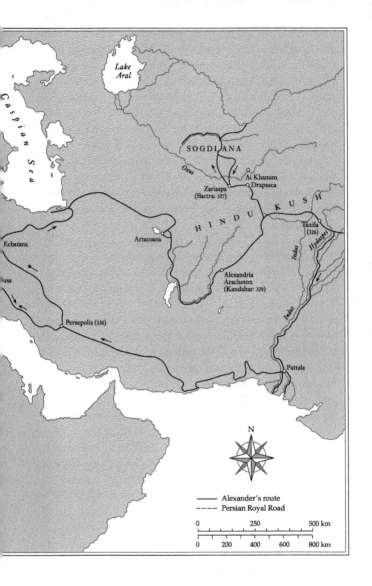

'India' (Pakistan/Kashmir), and not merely destroyed the old Persian empire in the process but also began to lay down the foundations of a new kind of personal territorial monarchy, a kingdom of 'Asia', with himself as the new-style part-Greek, part-orientalized monarch, worshipped spontaneously as a living god by many of his new oriental subjects. Greeks, however, found the idea of divine worship of him harder to get used to, and the expedition's official historian, Callisthenes (a relative of Alexander's old tutor Aristotle), whom Alexander had appointed himself, was also executed on his orders for treason, since he had objected to Alexander's demand that Greeks literally bow down to him in ceremonial obeisance—as if he were a Persian, not a Greek, Great King.

To stabilize his conquests strategically as he proceeded, as well as to unify his new kingdom culturally for the future, Alexander founded a number of Greek-speaking eponymous Alexandrias. There is much dispute both in the ancient sources and between ancient sources and modern historians over exactly how many new cities (whatever their name or nature) Alexander himself personally founded in all: perhaps only a dozen rather than the seventy-plus attributed to him in antiquity. Of those named after him, the majority are located in the further eastern reaches of his empire, established primarily for strategic reasons but with the potential, circumstances permitting, to grow into more settled, peaceful, and civilized Greek cities. But the first—after Alexandroupolis in northern Greece, which he had renamed rather than founded anew in 340—brand new Alexandria was established not in Europe, nor in Asia, but in Africa, in the Nile delta near that vast river's Canopic outlet into the Mediterranean.

Not only the first, the Egyptian Alexandria was also by far the most important of all his Alexandrias. In the winter of 332/1 (7 April 331, officially) Alexander personally supervised the laying out of its footprint, consulting as was his wont the 'best' soothsayers and seers at his disposal, headed by Aristander

of Telmessus (Fethiye in south-west Turkey today). He was careful
not to locate the city right on top of an existing Egyptian site,
for fear of alienating powerful native opinion, which he needed
urgently on his side—this was only six months or so before the
final, decisive battle with Darius III at Gaugamela in northern Iraq
in October 331. Instead, he located it next to one, called in Greek
Rhacotis—indeed, Alexandria itself was regularly referred to as 'by'
Egypt rather than 'in' Egypt, so much was it seen as an exceptional,
alien implant, with its own separate identity from the start, access
to which was very strictly controlled by the original Macedonian
and Greek settlers, some of whom were retired veterans,
others traders, yet others wideboys on the make. And below
them were, of course, an underclass of slaves of many ethnicities,
but also a lower order of free but unenfranchised Egyptians
and other incomers such as diaspora Jews. (It was for the
latter that the Hebrew Bible was first translated into Greek, later
known as the Septuagint, some time in the third century BCE.)

At first, during Alexander's lifetime and a little beyond,
Alexandria was the new capital of an imperial province, in
succession to the 'satrapy' of Egypt that the Persians had ruled
from 525 to 404 and again from 343/2 to 332, whose capital had
been the old Egyptian capital of Memphis. The powerful Egyptian
priesthood had never settled comfortably under the Achaemenid
yoke (as they saw it), and had periodically revolted. From 404
until 342, indeed, revolt had become a semi-permanent condition
under the last of the native Pharaohs, but Great King Artaxerxes
III had eventually reconquered the land, only for a successor,
Darius III, to lose it to Alexander ten years later. The Egyptians
generally welcomed in Alexander, as their enemies' enemy, but it
didn't take long for the old grievances against a foreign, imperial
power to surface again, and Alexander, it has to be said, was not at
his best in dealing with these new subjects tactfully. Rather he
sought to exploit his Egyptian connections mainly for personal
and propaganda purposes, having himself declared Pharaoh at
Memphis, and even hailed as the son of a god in Greek by

the chief priest of the oracle of Ammon (Amun) in the Siwah oasis many hundreds of kilometres to the west, on the borders with Libya.

In about 305 one of Alexander's most successful Macedonian generals, a companion since childhood called Ptolemy, whom Alexander had appointed governor of the province of Egypt, declared himself 'King' of the same territory, with Alexandria as his capital. What is more, he managed to found a lasting, if often troubled, dynasty. For almost three centuries thereafter, Alexandria was the capital of a 'Hellenistic' successor kingdom, the term 'Hellenistic' signifying Greek in culture and administration but significantly influenced by native culture, to the extent of there being some sort of fusion between the two, for example in the new dynastic religious cult of Serapis—a combination of the cult of Osiris (representing the spirit of the dead Pharaoh) and that of the Apis bull of Memphis.

Indeed, in the third century, thanks to its new Museum (shrine of the Nine Muses) and Library (the hugely enlarged collection is said to have incorporated, for example, even Aristotle's presumably large manuscript possessions), which Ptolemy I had at least planned for before he died in 283, Alexandria also became the capital of culture of the entire Greek world. Intellects of the calibre of Euclid, the mathematical genius, Eratosthenes (who among many other feats measured the earth's circumference to well within a perfectly acceptable margin of error), Archimedes (the maths genius and military inventor), Callimachus (chief Librarian, originally from Cyrene like Eratosthenes), and Theocritus (pastoral poet from Syracuse, composing at the Alexandrian court in the 270s under Ptolemy II) and many other luminaries too numerous to name individually graced the city's precincts.

The coexistence of 'scientists' and 'arts' specialists is noteworthy in itself, but harmony did not always reign supreme. A contemporary wit referred to the Museum as the 'birdcage of the Muses', implying that all sorts of highly competitive birds were kept cooped up there, without an agreed pecking order but with lots of mutual pecking going on. Even Ptolemy I himself had turned his hand to literature in old age, writing an apologetic account of 'my part in' Alexander's campaigns. This has not survived as such but it formed one of the bases of a good historical account that does, written by Arrian, a Greek from Nicomedea in Bithynia, in the second century CE. The lost memoirs trope has also given inspiration to at least one novelist (Valerio Massimo Manfredi) and one filmmaker (Oliver Stone, using Anthony Hopkins playing Ptolemy as his internal narrator).

Alexandria was thus the first Hellenistic *polis*, just as Alexander may fairly be designated as the first Hellenistic king. Would that archaeology could do anything like as much justice to the city's architectural wonders as the survival of literature has done to its intellectual achievements. But subsequent historical vicissitudes—hostile occupations, regime- and indeed culture-changes, and burnings deliberate and accidental—coupled with mighty forces of nature (earthquakes above all) have seen to it that much of Hellenistic Alexandria is either obliterated on land, or under water. Where, to take the most argued-over example, is Alexander's fabled tomb—the one built by Ptolemy I after he had hijacked Alexander's body (en route from Babylon for re-burial in Macedonia) and visited three centuries later in reverent homage by the first Roman Emperor, Augustus? Are his remains really now entombed in Venice, under St Mark's Cathedral, as a recent speculation would have it (the claim being that what were removed as supposedly the mortal remains of St Mark, an adopted Alexandrian, were actually those of Alexander)? Or is that just the sort of wild surmise to which the absence of a sound archaeological record can drive even the sanest of historical investigators?

Credit must at least be given to the underwater archaeologists such as Jacques-Yves Empereur and Franck Goddio who have recovered and are still recovering remarkable things from the deep off Alexandria and in areas up to 20 kilometres further east (ancient Heracleum?), housed now in the new National Museum of Alexandria. But even the most skilled of them will never recover enough of the Pharos lighthouse (100 metres tall, allegedly) designed for Ptolemy I or II by Sostratus of Cnidus, like the Mausoleum one of the canonical Seven Wonders of the Ancient World, or be able to reconstruct it persuasively, even on paper or in CGI, let alone hard reality.

Being a royal capital, in a brave new world of territorial monarchies (below), Alexandria could not function as just, let alone as just another, Greek *polis*. Laws passed here by the Ptolemies would have applied throughout Egypt, to natives as well as Greeks, as did the most impressive silver and gold imperial coinages—the first to depict a living ruler's image. But elsewhere in the post-Alexander Hellenistic world, which stretched from Greece and Egypt to Central Asia and Pakistan in today's terms, and from about 300 to 30 BCE, recent research has shown just how vigorous the *polis* remained as both a political and a cultural institution. For example, Greeks and Macedonians in the entourage or wake of Alexander took the *polis* to central Asia, to Bactria and Sogdia in what is now Afghanistan. The prime case is Ai Khanum ('Moon Woman' in the local Tadjik language), which is possibly ancient Alexandria in Sogdia. Reasonable doubts have been expressed about the extent and depth of the hellenization process here: were these not really just supersize forts from whose cultural delights the local 'barbarians' were rigorously debarred? Is not the architecture more local or Persian than Greek? Perhaps that might be argued as a general rule, though it would be hard to test it, and at any rate the posthumous hero-cult established there for the city's founder Cineas looks not at all different from that of, say, Timoleon in the centre of Syracuse.

On top of that, too, there are some staggeringly powerful and unanswerable individual pieces of evidence on the other side, in favour of hellenization, all the more powerful for coming from that most sensitive of cultural spheres—religion. Thus at the Takht-i-Sangin shrine 150 kilometres west of Ai Khanum on the Oxus (Syr-Darya) river one finds a dedication by the undoubtedly local man Atrosokes (whose name means something like 'having the force of the deity of fire'). It consists basically of a votive stone altar, inscribed with a dedication in Greek, atop which stands a bronze statuette of the old Silenus Marsyas playing a reeded double *aulos*! One wonders what Apollo (whom Marsyas fatally challenged to a musical duel in one myth, and lost his skin for being defeated) would have thought of that.

Had the Alexandrian poet C. P. Cavafy (1863–1933) still been alive when this altar was excavated, he for one would not have been at all discombobulated. Writing as if in (or from) the year 200 BCE, he imagines a Hellenistic Greek proudly declaring:

> We: the Alexandrians, the Antiochenes,
> the Seleucians, and the numerous
> other Hellenes of Egypt and Syria,
> and those in Media, and those in Persia, and so many others.
> With their extended dominions,
> and the diverse endeavours towards judicious adaptations.
> And the Greek *koinê* language—
> all the way to Bactria we carried it, to the peoples of India.

> (From 'In the Year 200 BC')

Conveniently for us as well, Cavafy here gives a short conspectus of almost the entire post-Alexander Hellenistic world. Antioch in Syria and Seleucia on the Tigris were the principal cities of the empire founded by Seleucus I the Conqueror, another general of Alexander's who as a privileged Companion of Alexander had taken an oriental wife at Alexander's request in 324 but unlike all the rest of the Companions had not rejected her after Alexander's death. He inherited or made his own most of the Asiatic component of Alexander's empire. The mention of Greeks in

Media and Persia (northern and southern Iran) is salutary, since they are often forgotten even by scholars. In Susa, indeed, the old administrative capital of the Persian Empire, we hear of performances or at least staged recitations of Euripides—something that would have been a commonplace in Alexandria, with its many theatres. The '*koinê* language' is the simplified form of Classical Greek, based chiefly on the Athenian dialect, that spread throughout the Middle East and indeed into part of what is today Pakistan. This was the Greek into which the Jewish Septuagint was translated, this the Greek of the Christian New Testament.

The one obvious omission from Cavafy's catalogue is the kingdom of the Attalid dynasty, a breakaway from the Seleucid empire in the first half of the third century. This was based on the old Aeolian Greek city of Pergamum in north-west Asia Minor. It was a member of this dynasty who paid for the large colonnaded portico in the Agora of Athens, replaced in the 1960s with a Rockefeller-funded simulacrum that houses today the museum and storeroom of the American School of Classical Studies. It is Pergamum too that gives us our word 'parchment', derived ultimately from the Latin 'pergamena charta', 'paper from Pergamum', meaning vellum.

But the international equilibrium that emerged by the middle of the third century was hard won, after two major intestine wars, and easily disturbed or lost. Much of Hellenistic Greek public political history, indeed, is but a wearisome catalogue of inter-dynastic wars (see Chronology). Thus the Ptolemies of Egypt fought a tedious and debilitating series of wars with the Seleucids of Asia, the intervening territory of Palestine and the Levant being both the prize and often the site of their conflicts. In old Greece the Antigonid dynasty of Macedon (descended from yet another of Alexander's generals, Antigonus the One-Eyed) periodically came down like a wolf to demonstrate who really was boss, as for example in 222 when Antigonus III Doson soundly defeated the radical, even revolutionary Spartan king Cleomenes III not far north of Sparta town at Sellasia. The boss of all bosses, *capo di capi*, was then still to emerge in all its *gloria*; indeed, in 216 Rome suffered a catastrophic defeat at Cannae at the hands of Carthaginian Hannibal. But very shortly after that Rome began its inexorable rise to supreme power and glory in the ancient Mediterranean world. Eventually, indeed, by 30 BCE it had included almost the entire Hellenistic world within its orbit as the eastern, Greek-speaking half of its empire; though its hold on what are now Iran and Iraq was brief and tenuous, and it never absorbed any part of Afghanistan or Pakistan.

The Greek historian Polybius of Megalopolis (*c*.200–120) set himself to chronicle and explain that magnum force. He began with Rome's pulling itself off the floor after its terrible defeat at Cannae and took the story as far as 145, by when Carthage had been destroyed and 'Macedonia' and 'Achaea' had been established as respectively a province and a protectorate within Rome's official imperial ambit. A dozen years later the old Pergamum kingdom followed suit, by bequest of its last ruler, under the grandiose title of the province of 'Asia'. Sixty years further on, Pompey the Great (emulating Alexander in his title as in much else) brought into the empire in effect the old Seleucid kingdom based on Syria, and most of the rest of Anatolia besides.

That left only Ptolemaic Egypt, but its acquisition was the consequence of an even more titanic struggle, for personal mastery of the entire Roman World: between, in the 'Western' corner, Gaius Julius Caesar Octavianus—Octavian, for short—adopted son and heir of Julius Caesar, the man who would surely have been Rome's first emperor but for his assassination in 44; and, in the 'Eastern' corner, Marcus Antonius—or Mark Antony, bigamous husband of the last of the Graeco-Macedonian Ptolemies, the cultivated and resourceful Queen Cleopatra VII. At the naval Battle of Actium in north-west Greece in 31 BCE Octavian's fleet decisively defeated that of

Map 6. Hellenistic World

Cleopatra and Antony, who both committed suicide back in
Alexandria rather than fall into Octavian's vengeful grasp. In 30
BCE Octavian turned Egypt into the equivalent of a Roman
imperial province, though it was governed by his direct
appointees, and members of the Senate were banned from

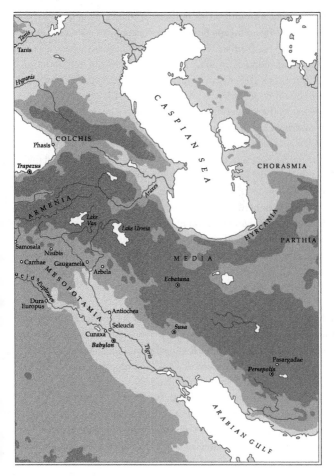

entering it without his express permission. With this
transformation of Egypt into a Roman dependency, the Romans
had completed the absorption of almost the entire post-Alexander
Hellenistic world into their massive empire (almost—they never
held Afghanistan, wisely enough perhaps, and only very briefly
occupied Iran).

But if ancient Alexandria was finished as an independent political entity, it was by no means finished intellectually or culturally in 30 BCE. Very far from it. The roll-call of intellectuals who graced Roman Alexandria is by no means clearly inferior to that of the city's illustrious Hellenistic incarnation. And perhaps pride of place should be accorded to another Ptolemy, Claudius Ptolemaeus the astronomer and geographer, who wrote at Alexandria between CE 146 and c.170. The medium onto which they transcribed their thoughts was a specially prepared product of the native Egyptian papyrus plant; always expensive, it had had to compete in the earlier Greek world with the cheaper writing media of bark, pottery, skin, and wax. But under the Roman dispensation papyrus comes into its own as our major source of evidence on social and cultural life in the ancient Greek world as a whole. Alexandria's soil and climate being too wet, the recovered papyri have come chiefly from further south in the Nile valley, from the Fayum region, and notably from the small and otherwise undistinguished town of Oxyrhynchus ('Sharp-nosed Fishville').

I, however, propose to end our very brief sketch with another of those very rare ancient Greek women who—like Queen Cleopatra most obviously—are on record as having an impact on what was a fundamentally male-oriented and male-dominated culture. Her name is Hypatia, and she was the daughter of a mathematician called Theon. She was not in fact the very first distinguished female Alexandrian mathematician—that accolade goes to Pandrosion, who perhaps invented a geometric construction to produce cube roots. Hypatia for her part wielded the astrolabe and the hydroscope with aplomb. But she owes her commemoration not only, alas, to her scientific brains, nor to her (allegedly) superior looks, but chiefly to the fact that she was murdered—or rather martyred—as a pagan, by a Christian mob possibly acting under orders of Bishop Cyril in CE 415. *Sic transit gloria classica.*

Chapter 12
Byzantion

Once the capital of imperial Rome; later the greatest city of Christendom, the richest city in the world, the spiritual head of the eastern Church, the treasure house of culture and art; then the opulent capital of Islam ... rising so superbly above three seas, looking towards Europe, Asia, and ocean, oriental, occidental ...

(From Rose Macaulay, *Pleasure of Ruins*, 1953)

Syracuse had been among the earliest of the new Greek settlements in the West. It took rather longer for Greeks to penetrate north and eastwards from the Aegean, up through the straits of Hellespont (Dardanelles) and Bosporus ('Oxen-ford'; the spelling Bosp*h*orus is a solecism) into the Black Sea. There were a number of reasons for this. The currents in the Hellespont are generally adverse, and the seasonal wind (now called *meltemi*) that blows hard from the north-east in the summer was fine for sailing ships coming down from the Black Sea—but exactly the opposite for those wanting to enter it. On the straits themselves lived potentially hostile 'natives', Thracians (European side) and Bithynians (Asiatic) in the case of the Bosporus. And what came to be called the Black Sea was known to the Greeks euphemistically as the 'Hospitable Sea', a superstitious alternative to the probably original 'Inhospitable Sea'. It was no surprise therefore that the Greeks established permanent settlements in this region crabwise, starting slowly with the Hellespont (Sestus, Abydus), then the Propontis (now Sea of Marmara: Cyzicus, Perinthus), and then the Bosporus.

And hereby hangs a tale that is curious, in a number of ways. The Greeks founded two cities here, facing each other—on the sites of what are today Istanbul (in Europe) and Kadiköy (in Asia). The mother city of (probably) both the new Bosporus cities was Megara in central Greece, a neighbour city, usually uneasily so, of Athens. Megara founded very few settlements abroad, but those it did found prospered exceedingly. In the West the foundation of Megara Hyblaea on the east coast of Sicily somewhere between 750 and 725 was among the first wave of new permanent Greek settlements, taking its name from a combination of the mother city's with that of a friendly local Sicel king, Hyblon. In the seventh century the Sicilian Megarians laid out a very early instance of a grid-planned civic centre, and the city's well-excavated architectural and funerary remains indicate wide trading contacts and a generally high level of prosperity. It was presumably this success story involving much emphasis on long-distance seaborne commerce that encouraged attempts to repeat it in the approaches to the Black Sea, where available agricultural land would be relatively restricted but the chance to exploit passing trade almost unlimited.

However, the first of the two cities was not established, as one would have predicted, on the European side, taking full advantage of the wonderful natural resource of the Golden Horn. It was established on the Asiatic side opposite and called Calchadon or Chalcedon—which gave rise to the lovely myth that these Megarian settlers must have been blind: blind to the attractions of the site of what became Byzantion. Today, the two are effectively parts of the same city, Istanbul, linked directly by ferry and indirectly by the magnificent bridge that straddles the Bosporus further north. This is not by any means the earliest such structure across the Bosporus on record—the honour for creating that goes to an ancient Greek architect and designer called Mandrocles, who came from the island of Samos and was in the employ of Persian Great King Darius I (reigned *c*.522–486). So pleased was Darius with his bridge of boats that he showered Mandrocles with presents. So pleased was Mandrocles with himself that he commissioned a painting of his creation which he dedicated to Hera, the patron goddess of his native island, accompanied by the following commemorative text (preserved by Herodotus):

> After spanning the Bosporus teeming with fish
> To Hera Mandrocles dedicated this
> To commemorate his work on the bridge of boats,
> Winning a crown for himself, and glory for Samos,
> By fulfilling the will of King Darius.

> (Trans. A. Purvis, slightly modified)

But whereas Mandrocles's bridge had been built from the Asiatic side for hostile purposes (to enable Darius's not all that successful invasion of Europe), and was dismantled once it had served its unique function, today's Bosporus bridge attracts traffic chiefly from the east, seeking to draw Asia into Europe, and supports a wholly peaceful intercourse.

After Byzantion's foundation—traditionally in either 688 or 657—we hear little or nothing of the city's politics until in 499 it revolted from its Persian suzerain as part of the 'Ionian Revolt' (499–494). Byzantion fortunately did not share the sad fate of the Revolt's ringleader, Miletus, but when the Persians came back in force in 480, crossing from Asia to Europe over the Hellespont by another bridge of boats, it could do nothing but send its required forces—to fight on the Persian side. More Greeks in fact then fought for or at least with the Persians than against them (see further Appendix). The loyalist Greeks' victories of 479, however, at Plataea and Mycale, presaged the liberation of Byzantion from the Persian empire. Indeed, for as long as Sparta maintained an interest in pursuing a campaign of liberation in Asia, Byzantion served as the allied HQ. But with the official recall of Regent Pausanias by Sparta (disobeying orders in a most un-Spartan way, he returned to Byzantion in a personal capacity and got caught up in accusations of pro-Persian sympathies), Athens assumed control and direction of the anti-Persian campaign; and Byzantion signed up as one of its many allies, agreeing to pay the high tribute of 15 silver talents per annum.

The importance of Byzantion to Athens lay chiefly in its ability to manage, and tax, the annual flow of ships trading in wheat and other staple goods from the black-earth lands of the Ukraine, south Russia, and the Crimea to Athens and other Aegean sites. A revealing documentary inscription found in Athens, set up probably in the early 420s, deals with relations between Athens on one side and the northern Greek city of Methone and the king of Macedon on the other. At two points there is mention of officials called 'Hellespontine Guards', based in Byzantion, who are charged with determining which Greek cities (other than Athens) were entitled to acquire how much of the shipped Black Sea grain at any time. Other sources speak of a fixed impost, levied by tax-collectors who were also based at Byzantion, on goods passing in both directions along the Bosporus.

Byzantion thus was a major node in the Athenians' imperial network. Small wonder that in the concluding phase of the Peloponnesian War and its immediate aftermath, when the Spartans at last acquired a decent fleet (thanks to massive Persian subventions), Byzantion featured as a principal war objective. An essential part of the Spartans' victory settlement of 404 was the disbandment of the Athenian empire, and the reduction of their once huge fleets of up to 300 ships to a maximum of twelve. But the Spartans had nothing against empire as such, and in order to service their own, newly expanded Aegean empire, they established the external office of *harmost* ('fixer'); one of the most important of these officials was based, naturally enough, at Byzantion.

And so the ding-dong over the possession of Byzantion between Sparta and a reviving Athens (thanks to Persia, switching sides against a now hostile Sparta) continued into the later 390s and early 380s—until Athens's naval power seemed to the Persians to have grown threateningly great again, all too reminiscent indeed of its fifth-century empire, including as it did control of Byzantion and reimposition therefrom of a trade-tax. Whereupon the Persians switched their support back to Sparta, which in the shape of Persian-friendly admiral Antalcidas managed to block off the Hellespont and thereby threaten Athens with starvation again (as in 405/4). There followed directly the King's Peace of 386, alternatively known as the Peace of Antalcidas, under which Byzantion was prised from Athens's grasp.

Yet there remained a strong pro-Athenian element in Byzantion, championed by the Athenians' official representative in the city called Philinus. It was probably he who led the Byzantine side in the negotiations that brought his city into alliance with Athens in 378/7, 'on the same terms as the city of the Chians'. The islanders of Chios had been loyal members of the Athenian empire for most of the fifth century, even though their constitution was oligarchic not democratic. But by 384, when they allied again with Athens, they did so as citizens of a democratic city, in sympathy with Athens ideologically now as well as strategically, and goaded by Sparta's flagrant abuse of the terms of the King's Peace (see Chapter 10). Byzantion was very likely in the same situation. And, as we have seen, Thebes too in 378 became a democracy, and in the summer of that same year these three democracies—Chios, Byzantion, and Thebes—joined with three other cities (Mytilene and Methymna on the island of Lesbos, and the island-city of Rhodes) as the six founder members of Athens's Second Naval League, an explicitly anti-Spartan alliance (whereas the First

League had been anti-Persian in origin and only much later became anti-Spartan).

To begin with, the new Athenian League prospered and grew hugely in numbers, counting some seventy-five states great and small at its maximum. This was because Athens offered leadership where it was wanted and genuinely did seem to be observing the pledges it had signed up to on oath, such as not to interfere with the property-rights or infringe any other legal privileges of its allied cities. However, from as early as 373 there is evidence that Athens progressively—or regressively—reneged on each one in turn, so that by 357 Byzantion was instrumental in fomenting what is known as the Social War, or War of the Allies (357–355). Another revolted ally in the mid-350s was, significantly, Chios, another founder-member, and Athens's defeat in 355 meant the effective end of the League as a power-unit.

Byzantion, finally (for our purposes), featured centrally in the rise of Philip of Macedon to supremacy. As early as 352 Philip had penetrated close to Byzantion in a hostile way, by a lightning march right across Thrace up to the western shore of the Propontis, at a place called Heraeum Teichos ('Hera's Fortification Wall'). But that was just sabre-rattling, showing the flag. Twelve years later, it was the real thing—Philip launched sieges first of Perinthus in the Propontis and then of Byzantion. Both, remarkably, failed—remarkably, not because either was a soft target, but because Philip was the pastmaster of siegecraft, and none of his previous sieges (most famously perhaps that of Amphipolis in 357) had failed. Since his principal opponent at this stage was Athens, what he was aiming to do was repeat what the Spartans had achieved in 405/4 and 387/6: choke off Athens's wheaten lifeline. If he could not achieve that by the seizure of those two key cities, then he would do it by even more direct action. Using Hierum at the mouth of the Black Sea as his base, he managed in that same summer of 340 to grab hold of an entire grain fleet headed for Athens.

Immediately, Athens had sufficient reserves and sufficient alternative grain sources not to be starved into submission (as in 405/4 and 387/6). But in the all too short run nothing was left for Athens but to risk all on a major direct confrontation with Philip in central Greece. The Battle of Chaeronea in Boeotia in autumn 338 was the consequence—a resounding triumph for Philip (and his 18-year-old son Alexander, commanding the crack Macedonian cavalry), but a total disaster for Thebes (placed thereafter under a Macedonian garrison), for Athens (not garrisoned, but neutralized), and, at first, for Philip's principal Athenian enemy, the very wealthy but convinced ideological democrat Demosthenes.

To Demosthenes Philip was not only a barbarian but a walking disaster for the future of true—enlightened, democratic, cultivated—Hellenism. Until the end of his days he engaged in an unceasing struggle to rouse the Athenians to outright revolt against their Macedonian overlord. But when an opportunity finally came, in 323–322, with the death of Alexander, and the Athenians did lead a revolt involving some twenty Greek cities, they fared no better than they had in 338 militarily speaking, and far far worse politically, since Macedon under its new hardline rulers decided they had had enough of Athens's pesky 'People-Power' and terminated it forthwith. Democracy in ancient Greece did not quite breathe its last in 322 but it was a relatively feeble thing thereafter. Demosthenes symbolically compassed his own end by taking poison on the island of Calaurea, today's Poros, evading thereby a worse fate of torture and murder at the hands of his pro-Macedonian enemies.

Chapter 13
Epilogue

Captive Greece (Graecia capta) *took its fierce conqueror captive.*

(Horace, d. 8 BCE)

Horace's famous *Graecia capta* epigram was a huge compliment—and a fundamentally accurate one. Indeed, it is ultimately thanks to the Romans' decision to declare themselves the cultural legatees of classical Greece that we in turn may echo Shelley's hyperbolic but in some sense defensible claim that 'We are all Greeks'. However, between the Romans and the Romantics—and Us—stood two seemingly immovable obstacles.

The first, somewhat paradoxically, were the Greeks of Byzantium and the Byzantine world, who persisted in calling themselves 'Romans' in preference to 'Hellenes', not least because they were Christians, whereas 'Hellenes', thanks to the preachings and prejudices of the ex-Jewish Christian authors of the New Testament—written, ironically, in Greek—had acquired the connotation of 'pagans' (see Glossary).

Second, there was the formidable Ottoman empire, which first put paid to Byzantium (the empire), then expunged the name of

Constantinople, as Byzantion (the city) had long become known, in favour of Istanbul, and then extended their Muslim empire from Algeria via Syria and Egypt right round to Hungary. As the mightiest of the Ottoman monarchs, Süleyman the Magnificent, put it (in a treaty with the Habsburg emperor) in 1565, a little over a century after the termination of the Byzantine world:

> I ... am Sultan of Sultans of East and West, Emperor and Sultan of the Black Sea and the Mediterranean ... the undisputed champion of the Cosmos ... Sultan Süleyman, son of Sultan Selim.

From his perspective, the glory that had been Greece (to paraphrase Edgar Allan Poe) as late as the second century CE must have seemed very far away indeed. That fertile century had witnessed the heyday of the so-called 'Second Sophistic': a revival of Hellenism, fostered by such philhellenic Roman emperors as Hadrian and his adopted grandson Marcus Aurelius, and written up by such ornaments of it as Plutarch, Arrian, and Pausanias. True, this had been a nostalgic sort of Hellenism, indeed in Hadrian's case Panhellenism; but it had been none the less real or potent for that. The very last spark, or gasp, of it appeared a couple of centuries later, with the brief reign of another emperor, Julian the Apostate (reigned 361–3); he was so called because, though brought up an orthodox Christian, he had retro-converted to an intellectual form of paganism. But, by his day, to be a philhellene pagan or polytheist was to be a reactionary, raging impotently against the dying of the light of the pagan gods and their supersession by the one true god of Catholic (universal) Orthodox (correct-belief) Monotheism (one-god-ism). The very incarnation of the latter creed in its human, mundane form was the first overtly Christian Roman Emperor, Constantine the Great (reigned 312–37).

Constantine is the last of our Founders of cities. So far in this book we have spanned the entire potential range of types of founders: from the mythical Minos (Cnossos), Theseus (Athens), Cadmus

(Thebes), and the descendants of Heracles (Sparta), through the entirely human and historical (but posthumously heroized) colony-founders of Massalia, Syracuse, and Byzantion, acting on behalf of the metropoleis of Phocaea, Corinth, and Megara respectively, to the heroized and divinized King Alexander the Great (Alexandria). Constantine came from what is now Nis in Serbia, a soldier-emperor with a Roman not Greek name. Yet he chose in 324 to establish a new, Greek, eastern capital for the Empire, astride the Bosporus strait separating the landmasses of Europe and Asia, dividing East from West.

That capital, dedicated on 11 May CE/AD 330, he had called after himself, Constantinoupolis, the *polis* of Constantine, following a long imperial naming tradition going back to Philip of Macedon (Philippopolis, modern Plovdiv in Bulgaria) and his son Alexander (first Alexandroupolis in what is today Greek Thrace, then a spate or spasm of Alexandrias, most famously that in Egypt: above, Chapter 11). But Constantinople had originally been Byzantion, founded as such, as we have seen above, in the earlier seventh century BCE. And from the mid-fifteenth century it has been Istanbul—perhaps a Turkish corruption of a Greek phrase including the word *polis*—but that is another story. At least Ottoman Sultan Mehmet the Conqueror, who in 1453 ended the millennium-long reign of Byzantium (the civilization and epoch), had the grace to speak and write and read Greek, indeed prided himself on doing so. Even the magnificent Süleyman spoke, as we saw, of a 'cosmos', a thoroughly Greek term meaning originally 'orderliness'. And his principal court architect, Sinan, one of the very greatest architects there has ever been, not just of Ottoman Islam, was very likely by birth a Byzantine Greek.

In November 324, when Roman Emperor Constantine founded Constantinople as his new Eastern capital, the Greeks repaid Horace's compliment, in spades (if I may use a suitably constructional metaphor). For thereafter all Byzantine Greeks were 'Romans', and it was therefore as 'Praetorian Prefect' that, a century or so later, following a devastating earthquake, Flavius Constantinus oversaw the rebuilding of the massive city-walls under the reign of Emperor Theodosius II. A laconic and clearly legible inscription on a marble slab still *in situ* boasts, in three rough hexameter verses:

By Theodosius's command in less than two months
Constantinus triumphantly built these strong walls.
So swiftly such a secure citadel [even] Pallas could hardly build.

Like Rome, Constantinople was built on seven hills. But constructional rivalry might extend even to a derogatory comparison with the Acropolis of Athens and its patron goddess Pallas Athena—a clearcut case of hubris, surely!

Right down to Mehmet II's conquest in 1453 of what was left of the Byzantine Empire, the Byzantines stubbornly called themselves 'Romans'; indeed, still today one word for the essential quality of Greekness is *Romiosyni*—'Roman-ness' (the title of a famous modern poem by Yannis Ritsos, set to music by Mikis Theodorakis). Yet the city of Byzantium, or rather Byzantion, as we have seen, also takes us back—almost—to the beginning of our story of ancient Greece and historical Greek civilization. Moreover, in the process of founding and establishing their new colonial *polis* in largely alien territory, the Byzantines subjected the local Bithynians to a status of serfdom comparable to that suffered by the Helots of the Spartans. Yet again we see Freedom and Slavery, Savagery and Civilization advance hand in hand in the remarkable history of the ancient Hellenes.

The history of Byzantium (the epoch, the civilization) has often suffered by comparison with that of Classical, even Archaic or Hellenistic Greece. By no means the most original, but probably the most tart, expression of this negative point of view is to be found in Edward Gibbon's magnificently comprehensive

127

Decline and Fall of the Roman Empire (chapter 48, first published in 1788):

> the subjects of the Byzantine empire, who assume and dishonour the names both of Greeks and Romans, present a dead uniformity of abject vices, which are neither softened by the weakness of humanity, nor animated by the vigour of memorable crimes.

Ouch! We note that the Byzantines did not suffer merely from vices, but from 'abject' vices, the uniformity of which was not simply uniform but 'dead'. Above all, the Byzantines' greatest failing was political, that theirs was not a free civilization. However, what Gibbon's immediately preceding unqualified paean to the free citizens of ancient Athens failed to observe was that such political freedom was conditional, indeed somehow based, directly or indirectly, upon the labours of a far larger multitude of unfree chattel slaves; just as the heroism of the Spartans at Thermopylae and Plataea, which had so signally contributed to keeping Greece free (from 'barbarian', Persian domination), was purchased at the expense of the hereditary servitude of even larger numbers of men and women, Helots as they were derogatorily labelled, who—unlike the chattels of the Athenians—were themselves Greeks, with lively if no doubt inaccurate collective memories of the 'good old days' when they too had been free.

This dialectic reminds us that, although the culture of the pre-Hellenistic and (through Rome) the Hellenistic Greeks is one of the West's most important cultural taproots, whence springs our borrowing of 'politics', 'democracy', and much else from them, yet their culture and politics were also in important respects not just very different from but also frankly alien, desperately foreign—at any rate since the successful Abolitionism of the 1830s—to our ways of behaving and thinking: in a word, 'other'.

One reason indeed for continuing to study ancient Greek civilization is precisely to try to take the measure of this difference or 'otherness', to balance it against what we have—or think we have—in common with them culturally speaking. Let me move to a conclusion by accentuating the positive aspects of our Hellenic legacy, first by examining briefly two famous aphorisms: one collective, impersonal, and, because of its location, of divine origin; the other attributed to one specific human being in an all too human context. Together, these two illustrate well, I think, both the attractive seeming similarity, and the sharp alterity of the Greeks' legacy.

Gnôthi seauton ('know yourself') was one of the (three) famous injunctions inscribed on the temple of Apollo at Delphi, the spiritual 'navel' of the ancient Greeks' cosmos (see Appendix). An important as well as interesting way for us today to carry out that injunction is to try—like our Roman cultural ancestors before us—to get to know what made the Greeks tick, to try at least to understand though not necessarily to explain completely their most fundamental social and cultural practices. Politics, I shall argue below, is of the essence in that process of understanding, even if of a very different kind from any that we in the liberal West may be used to.

The other aphorism goes like this: 'the unexamined life is for a human being not worth living'. It is credited to Socrates *in extremis* by his greatest pupil, Plato, in his version of the *Apology* (Defence Speech) that Socrates supposedly delivered during his trial before a democratic People's Court at Athens in 399 BCE (see Chapter 8). It is characteristic of Greek dialectical thought that that aphorism is both perfectly compatible with, indeed complementary to, the Delphic maxim discussed above and also potentially violently contradictory of it. For, on the one hand (to use the characteristic ancient Greek form of antithesis, signalled by the particles 'men' and 'de'), the outcome of the process of getting to know oneself might be the convinced self-knowledge that one was human, and not divine, and therefore bound to respect and observe unquestioningly and unconditionally the laws and ordinances imposed by 'the divine' on mere weak, feeble, and above all mortal humans. (That was to be the line followed and imposed by Christian Byzantine emperor Justinian, when in CE 529 he ordered to be closed all Greek schools of philosophical, that is originally pre-Christian, teaching, most famously the Academy of Athens.) On the other hand ('de'), it might be interpreted at its maximum opposite stretch to mean living a life in which one questioned absolutely everything, not least or especially human-made conventions and customs (for which the Greeks used the same word, *nomos*, as they used for 'laws', positive legal enactments), and not excluding therefore questioning even conventional belief in the very existence, let alone peremptory authority, of the divine.

Such contests (*agônes*) of interpretation were particularly, though not exclusively, a feature of ancient Greek democratic societies and cultures such as those of Athens and Syracuse in the Classical period. But competitiveness (Greek *agônia*) is by no means an ancient Greek prerogative. For all I know, there may be readers of this book who wish to take issue with or possibly derogate some part or even the whole of it. But to them, and indeed any others, I should like in closing to recommend the very opposite of an excommunication or excoriation—an encomium, or paean, if admittedly a rather double-edged one.

In about 300 CE a Greek called Menander nicknamed Rhêtôr ('the Orator') composed a short treatise on how to praise a *polis*. I quote from Mogens Hansen's own book of that title (*Polis*, p. 158 n.12):

> The urban aspects of the *polis* are emphasised, but when it comes to
> the political achievements and the constitution of the *polis*,
> Menander admits that there is no longer much to be said here,
> because all Roman *poleis* are now governed by one *polis*, sc. Rome!

How are the mighty prophets fallen—in little over a generation's time, another *polis* would arise, a new Rome mightier by far (then, in the fourth century of our era) than the old one: namely, Byzantion/ Constantinople, the new capital of Roman Emperor Constantine the Great (died 337). The site was brilliantly chosen, bestriding as it did the Europe–Asia confluence and throwing down a challenge both to the old Roman world in the West and to the various threats to Roman suzerainty emanating from the Orient, 'barbarian' or otherwise.

Its foundation constitutes also as neat an exemplification as one could wish for of the quasi-law enunciated by Herodotus (book 1, chapter 5) some seven centuries or so earlier:

> I shall ... proceed with the rest of my story recounting cities (*poleis*)
> both lesser and greater, since many of those that are great in my
> own time were inferior before.

Ancient Greek Byzantion had been founded about a millennium earlier and had risen to significance, if not greatness, owing to its energetic exploitation both of the local Bithynians' labour power and of its site's unparalleled opportunities for taxing trade passing through the Bosporus. But the new Byzantion differed crucially from its predecessor not only in being an imperial capital but in being the capital of a Christian—Orthodox and Catholic ('universal')—empire. In CE 325 at Nicaea (Iznik) Constantine summoned a Council of Bishops to place the stamp of monotheist orthodoxy—the Nicene creed—on his mundane world. The old 'pagan' gods were by no means entirely dead yet—indeed they still have their adherents to this day; but the old relatively tolerant and inclusive pagan establishment was being compelled to give way before an exclusive, dogmatic creed that could countenance such acts as the murder of Hypatia in Alexandria, a murder at which the Bishop of that city seems to have connived. Of course, it is open to argument whether such murders of pagans by Christians and (more common still) of Christians by other Christians were in

131

any sense worse than those of citizens by fellow-citizens in the bloody *staseis* (such as the 'Clubbing' at Argos) that disfigured Classical Greek antiquity. But at any rate it is clear that the old Greek *polis*—a city of (many) gods as well as of men—was a thing of the past.

Alexandria, however, retains its fascination today, if largely for nostalgic reasons, in the classicizing poems of the native poet C. P. Cavafy (1863–1933), one of which is called 'The City' (*Hê Polis*), in the idiosyncratic 'History and Guide' by E. M. Forster (1922), and in the fictionalized pages of Lawrence Durrell (classically inspired author of the *Alexandria Quartet*, 1957–60, in which Cavafy is referred to as 'the old Poet of the city'), above all. One exception to that rule of nostalgia is the magnificent new Library of Alexandria, a 'virtual' facility of Norwegian design, which is as much of our present age as the original was of the ancient Greeks' present in 200 BCE, 2,200 years ago.

The new Library's website tells us that 'it is dedicated to recapture the spirit of openness and scholarship of the original Bibliotheca Alexandrina', though actually that is the Latin not the Greek form of its name, and the original spirit of the scholarship that went on in the Museum to which it was attached was, as we have seen, characterized at least as much by *odium academicum* as by the free and open exchange of ideas and knowledge. All the same, openness is indeed a fair representation of the ancient Greek ideal, and if there is one message that I should like to bring to the fore in the conclusion of this very short introduction to ancient Greece by way of a small selection from its myriad cities, it is precisely that of openness, the openness of debate.

Our word 'politics' comes from the ancient Greek neuter plural adjective *politika* meaning 'matters relating to the *polis*' (as used, most famously, for Aristotle's greatest work of political sociology and political theory, composed in the 330s and 320s). For the Greeks, politics happened centre-stage—'towards the middle' (*es *meson*), as they literally put it. Public affairs, that is to say, were intended to be not just of concern to, but physically decided by, the citizenry as a whole, meeting 'towards the middle' to discuss, debate, and thrash out what they took, rightly or wrongly, to be the common good, the public interest of the city and its citizens. True, women were allowed no part of this communal political enterprise of decision-making; true, there were an awful lot of slaves or subjugated serf-like workers in or rather outside most of the cities, providing the citizens on the inside with the indispensable leisure (*skholē*, whence our 'school') to do politics as they saw fit; true, it was only in a pretty radical democracy such as Athens that most of the ordinary poor male citizens really did get the chance regularly to decide the issues for themselves; and true too, finally, Greek citizens had an unfortunate tendency to resort quite frequently to outright civil war (*stasis*) to settle their internal differences, and *phthonos* (envy) rather than friendship ruled rather too frequently in relations between Greek cities. And yet, even as an ideal that was quite often not well instantiated, Greek politics deserve at least our concentrated attention, and often enough, I would say, our respect, if not imitation. That at all events is for me a working definition of what 'civilization' is—a civilization essentially of cities.

Appendix

The Panhellenic Sanctuaries

By definition, the 'Panhellenic' ('all-Greek' but not necessarily only-Greek) religious sanctuaries, of which the chief two were Olympia and Delphi, were inter-state rather than city sanctuaries. But the cities by no means buried their separate political identities when they came together, collectively or individually, officially or unofficially, to explore or exploit those two numinous, ultimately religious spaces. At Olympia, for example, eleven cities—among them Syracuse and Byzantion (Massalia did likewise at Delphi)—erected 'Treasuries' both to mark out and put their mark on their own special portion of that common Greek soil but also to advertise their standing—or at any rate self-perception—within the quarrelsome Greek family of cities. At Delphi, to take only the classic example, Sparta and Argos competed as visually and visibly as was humanly possible by erecting counter-monuments side-by-side at the very entrance to the Sacred Way leading up to the main display centre of the sanctuary around the Temple of Apollo (on which were engraved the three Delphic maxims, honoured as much in the breach as the observance: 'Know thyself', 'Nothing in excess', and 'Never go surety'). More genuinely harmonious, indeed more spiritually religious, were the Mysteries at Eleusis, participants in which were known as *mystae* (Glossary), but these were open to Greek-speaking non-Greeks as well as to Greeks, and even to slaves, besides being located within the territory of a major city, Athens.

8. Olympia—model

Olympia emerged first in the eleventh to tenth centuries BCE as a more than purely local site for worship, attested materially by multiple individual offerings of terracotta and bronze figurines representing animals and humans as well as the titular god, Olympian Zeus. What may have given a further boost to Olympia's wider than purely local or regional appeal was the presence of an oracular shrine, dedicated like the sanctuary as a whole to Zeus, whose surname of 'Olympian' (from Mount Olympus in Macedonia, the highest in Greece, at well over 3,000 metres) gave its name to the location. But it was the establishment here, traditionally in 776 BCE, of competitive athletic games—'competitive' reflects the Greek word *agônes*, 'contests'; 'athletic' comes from the Greek *athla* meaning 'prizes'—that set Olympia on course for first national, then international, and now global fame. (I write when the 2008 Beijing Olympics are still a recent memory, but must add that the notion of a 'Paralympics' would have astonished the ancient Greeks, who rather despised the less than physically perfect, as would the notion of silver and bronze as well as gold medals, if slightly less so.) And one reason why the ultimately five-day Games, attracting perhaps as many as 40,000 spectators, could be held here was spelled out in the first line of the first of Pindar's Olympian Odes: 'water is best'. The Olympia area, at the junction of the Alpheius and Cladeus rivers, was unusually aqueous for southern Greece.

Formally, as noted, Olympia belonged to all Greeks. But it was just the one city, medium-size Elis nearby, that managed the quadrennial Games all by itself, from the sending out of sacred ambassadors to declare the sacred truce (*ekekheiria*, literally 'armistice') before the five-day festival to the final animal sacrifice to Zeus to celebrate its conclusion. And it was Elis too, therefore, that appointed from among its own citizens the managing board of officials proudly known as *Hellanodikai* or 'Judges of the Greeks'. Here is part of a law promulgated in *c.*500 BCE by the city of Elis and displayed publicly on a bronze tablet within the sacred

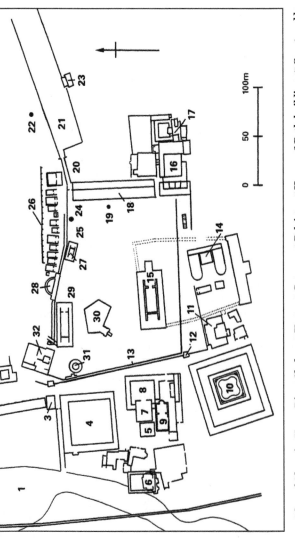

9. Plan of Olympia. Key: 1 River Cladeus 2 Xystos 3 Gateway 4 Palaistra 5 Heroon 6 Bath-buildings 7 Courtyard house 8 Residential house 9 'Workshop of Pheidias' 10 Leonidaion 11 Club-house 12 Processional entrance 13 Wall 14 Bouleuterion 15 Temple of Zeus 16 House of Nero 17 Roman baths 18 Doric colonnade 19 Honorific monument 20 Secret entrance 21 Stadium 22 Altar 23 Umpires' stand 24 Bases 25 Terrace 26 Treasuries 27 Metroon 28 Nymphaion 29 Temple of Hera 30 Precinct of Pelops 31 Philippeion 32 Prytaneion

enclosure (the Altis) at Olympia; it prescribes immunity and protection for some sorts of accused persons:

> The *rhêtra* [pronouncement] of the Eleans.... If anyone makes a charge against them [certain accused], he shall be prosecuted as in (the case of) an Elean. If he who holds the highest office and the kings [other officials] do not exact the fines, each one who fails to exact them shall pay a fine of 10 minas [one tenth of a talent, a substantial sum] consecrated to Olympian Zeus. The *hellênodikas* and the *damiorgoi* [Public Workers board] shall enforce the other fines ... The tablet sacred at Olympia.

> (Trans. M. Dillon and L. Garland, *Ancient Greece: Social and Historical Documents from Archaic Times to the Death of Socrates*, 1994, 307, no. 10.28, slightly modified)

There we find a nice, thoroughly ancient Greek, combination of the sacred and the profane, the political and the religious. Olympia and the Olympic Games were to flourish on that basis for well over 1,000 years. A work of the third century CE, a purported biography of a first-century Greek philosopher called Apollonius of Tyana, closes with a vignette of the great man holding court at Olympia for no fewer than forty days; there he was visited, his biographer says, by elite youths and men from Elis, Sparta, Corinth, Megara, Boeotia, and from as far afield as Phocis and Thessaly. The pagan gods were clearly not yet dead then. But in CE 395 Orthodox Christian Byzantine Emperor Theodosius I ordered all 'pagan' celebrations to be abolished, for ever, and that was indeed the end of the Games, though not of paganism as such.

The sanctuary at Delphi in Phocis was sacred to one of Zeus's many sons, Apollo, and the principal site for oracular consultations in the entire Greek world. A famous case of competitive oracular consultation involved a Spartan king in 388 BCE first securing the response he wanted from Zeus's oracle at Olympia and then asking Apollo at Delphi whether he 'agreed with his father'—an offer not even mighty Apollo could decently refuse! Delphi means 'wombs', and for the Greeks it counted as the navel (*omphalos*) of the entire cosmos—its central position determined mythologically when Zeus released two eagles to fly round the world in opposite directions and they met at Delphi, precisely.

Its exact origins as a Panhellenic sanctuary are, however, like those of Olympia, lost in the mists of the Greek Dark Age (eleventh to ninth centuries BCE), but one distinctive factor that may account in part for Delphi's spectacular emergence in the eighth century was its cardinal enabling role in the process of overseas colonization. As we noted in the Miletus chapter, Delphic Apollo was the god of Greek colonization. By the 730s at the latest, it was generally agreed that any act of creating a new overseas foundation in Sicily required the explicit prior approval and authorization of Delphic Apollo, to whom a common—to all Greek settlers, that is—shrine was established at Sicilian Naxus; and by the 630s, a century later, Apollo could feel sufficiently confident of his pre-eminent status to order a consultant from the parched Cycladic island of Thera (Santorini today) to found a city on a spot (Cyrene, in today's Libya) that he, Apollo—though not the consultant—knew about, because (so the god claimed in an 'automatic', i.e. unsolicited, response) he had already been there himself...

Delphi, like Olympia, was also the location of quadrennial Panhellenic Games (instituted, however, a couple of centuries later, in 582), which included musical and poetical as well as athletic and equestrian contests. The Games were managed by a special, permanently constituted Council, known as an Amphictiony, which was composed of representatives from all the main cultural and geographical divisions of Greece, but weighted towards representatives from the fairly local region of Thessaly. In 480 the sanctuary was menaced and—probably—desecrated by the Persians, though the Delphic priesthood stoutly maintained that Apollo had kept it inviolate, just as they maintained—equally

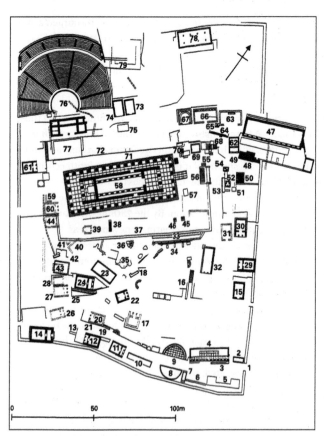

10. Plan of the Sanctuary of Apollo at Delphi. Key: 1 Entrance 2 Base
of the bull of Corcyra 3 Bases of the Arcadians 4 Stoa 5 Monument of
the Admirals 6 Site of Miltiades monument 7 Base of the Trojan horse
of the Argives 8 Base of the Seven and Epigones 9 Monument of the
kings of Argos 10 Base of the Tarentines 11 Treasury of the Sicyonians
12 Treasury of the Siphnians 13 Base of Liparaeans 14 Treasury of the
Thebans 15 Treasury 16 Staircase 17 Treasury 18 Base of the Boeotians
19 Base of the Aetolians 20–21 Treasury and terrace of the Megarians
22 Treasury of the Cnidians 23 Council-house 24 Treasury of the
Athenians 25 Base of Marathon 26 Treasury of 'The Boeotians'
27 Treasury 28 Treasury 29 Treasury of the Cyrenaeans 30 Treasury

implausibly—that they had taken a robustly Hellenic attitude of uncompromising opposition to the barbarian invader.

At all events, it was Delphi rather than Olympia that was selected as the site for the erection by 'the Hellenes' (this was what members of the allied resistance against Persia called themselves) of the major official victory-monument for the Graeco-Persian Wars of 480–479. This was done in spite of all the surrounding evidence the sanctuary site offered of a near-permanent state of internecine warfare between Greek cities: for Delphi was the location of choice for cities to display their spoils of war, as proof of Apollo's past special favour towards them, and in the hopes of his future aid and comfort. Olympia did of course commemorate the victory over the Persians too, but Nemea, controller of another sanctuary of Zeus where Panhellenic Games were held, did not do so—perhaps because it preferred to keep on good terms with its more powerful near-neighbour Argos, which had been professedly 'neutral' in the war.

10. (*cont.*) 'of Brasidas and the Acanthians' 31 Treasury 32 Treasury of the Corinthians 33 Stoa of the Athenians 34 Halos 35 Rock of the Sibyl 36 Column and sphinx of the Naxians 37 Polygonal wall 38 Fountain 'of the Muses' 39 'Shrine of Gê', 40–41 *Oikoi* 42 Fountain of the Asclepieum 43 Treasury under the Asclepieum 44 Treasury 45 Approximate site of the pillar of Messene 46 Suggested site of the black limestone column 47 Stoa of Attalus 48 Pillar of Eumenes II 49 Pillar of Attalus I 50 Chariot of Helios 51 Serpent column 52 Crotonian base 53 Base of the Tarentines 54 Location of the Apollo of Salamis 55 Aetolian column of Eumenes II 56 Altar of Apollo 57 Column of Aemilius Paulus 58 Temple of Apollo 59 *Oikos* 60 Treasury 61 Treasury 62 Treasury 63 Precinct and unfinished base 64 Base of Corcyra 65 Base of acanthus column 66 Base of Daochus 67 Semicircular base 68 Tripods of Gelon and Hieron 69 Base of 'Apollo Sitalcas' 70 Pillar of Prusias 71 Niche used as a fountain 72 Ischegaon 73 Treasury of the theatre 74 Treasury of the theatre 75 *Oikos* 76 Theatre 77 Niche of Craterus 78 Leschê of the Cnidians 79 Unidentified monument

The victory-monument consisted of a golden tripod cauldron borne aloft by a bronze column about 6 metres high set on a stone base, the column taking the form of coils topped by snakes' heads—whence the compendious name for the whole object of 'The Serpent Column'. On the coils of the column are inscribed, in the local Delphian dialectal forms of the Greek alphabet, the names of 'these [who] fought the war', as the prescript laconically puts it: that is, the cities and regional entities that agreed on oath to resist the Persians—of which there were a mere thirty-one (out of the 700 or so *poleis* in mainland Greece and the Aegean alone!). So much for the notion of 'the Greeks', all of them, resisting 'the Persians'...Actually, more Greeks fought on the Persian than the Greek side.

The list is organized in groups of three and headed by 'Lacedaemonians' (Spartans), 'Athenians', and 'Corinthians'. Twenty-nine of the thirty-one named are individual *poleis*, and they include historical Mycenae (then still extant, but destined to be destroyed utterly by Argos little over a decade later). Another ten besides Sparta, Corinth, and Mycenae were located in the Peloponnese, another seven besides Athens in central Greece north of the Corinthian isthmus. The two that were not individual *poleis* were the *ethnos* (people) of the Malians (though ironically it was a Malian, Ephialtes, who betrayed the Greeks at Thermopylae to Xerxes for money—and thus gave his name to the modern Greek word for 'nightmare') and the 'Ceans', a collective name for the four *poleis* situated on the island of Ceos not far off the Attic east coast. Also islanders were the men of Aegina (Saronic Gulf), Tenos, Naxos, Cythnos, and Siphnos (Cyclades), Eretria, Chalcis, and Styria (Euboea), and Leucas (an all-but island, off the west coast of central Greece). Notably, even this very short list was selective—it should surely also have included at least Croton (in 'Great Greece', that is, south Italy), Palê (on the island of Cephallenia), Seriphos (Cycladic island), and the Opuntian (East) Locrians (a central Greek *ethnos*, like the Malians). But such

11. Byzantion, Hippodrome (Serpent Column). The 'Serpent Column' – a bronze column representing the coils of a three-headed serpent, supporting a golden cauldron – was originally erected at Delphi to celebrate the Greeks' victory over Persia in 479 BC but removed eight centuries later to the Hippodrome of Constantinople

invidious selectivity was ever the case with Panhellenism, a competitive as much as it was a co-operative ideological signifier.

The cauldron was sacrilegiously melted down in the 350s BCE by the local Greeks of the district of Phocis within which Delphi lay; the Phocians were then engaged in a fierce struggle (ironically labelled a 'Sacred' War) with King Philip II of Macedon for control of Delphi and were in dire need of precious metal to pay foreign (other-Greek) mercenaries in coin or bullion. But all has not been quite lost yet. Some of the Serpent Column's stone base survives to this day at Delphi. And what is left of the serpentine bronze column itself is to be found, a world away, in Istanbul, to be precise in what was the hippodrome (horse-race stadium) of ancient Constantinople (Fig. 11). How it got there is another story, for another book; but we may conclude this one by observing that in this very short study of the Ancient Greeks' civilization of cities all roads, it seems, lead to (the new) Rome—and thence, via a War of Independence from Ottoman Turkey, to the new Greece.

Further Reading

I have been deliberately selective here. Apart from in the first, 'General' section, I have usually restricted my recommendations to just one or two books or accessible articles, written in English. Suggestions for even further further reading are often given in the works cited below, especially in my *Cambridge Illustrated History of Ancient Greece* ('Further Reading', pp. 371–3).

Special mention, however, must be made at the outset of Kathleen Freeman's *Greek City-States*, first published in 1950 by the long defunct Macdonald & Co. (Publishers) Ltd. of Ludgate Hill in the City of London. Quite by chance, after I had completed in Cambridge the research for and the writing up of this book, I stumbled across a second-hand copy of Freeman's book in the famous Strand Bookshop on Broadway in New York City (where I hold a visiting position at New York University, as Hellenic Parliament Global Distinguished Professor in the Theory and History of Democracy). Or rather—I stumbled across it again: for, as I at once recognized, this had been the set textbook for a class on ancient Greek history that I had taken at the University of California at Santa Barbara in the spring semester of 1965, under Professor Stylianos Spyridakis (now of the University of California at Davis).

Freeman opens with a quotation from Max Cary's *The Geographic Background of Greek and Roman History* (Oxford University Press, 1949): 'Geographic factors count for much in history; but personality is an even greater force.' Well, that, in my view, depends ... But I completely agree, of course, with what Freeman herself claims in her Preface, that 'If the Greek world is really to be understood we must know not only about Athens and Sparta, but about the islands of the Aegean Sea, the Greek cities of Sicily and Italy and Asia Minor, and the other cities of mainland Greece'; and with her decision therefore to cast her book in the form of a series of individual city-studies. Freeman's book is about twice as long as this one, yet she deals with just nine cities (Thurii, Acragas, Corinth, Miletus, Cyrene, Seriphos, Abdera, Massalia, and Byzantion). We agree on only three of those choices (Chapters 5, 6, and 12, above), and I did not have the brass neck to deny chapters to Athens and Sparta. Moreover, almost sixty years of scholarship (especially by the Copenhagen POLIS Centre) have outmoded a considerable amount of what she says, and even in 1950 not everything she wrote was entirely accurate or persuasive. All the same, it is a pleasure to salute a forerunner and, for all I know, an unconscious inspiration to me from over four decades back.

General

Reference

Barrington Atlas of the Greek and Roman World, ed. R. Talbert (Princeton University Press, 2000; available also as CDRom).
The Cambridge Dictionary of Greek Civilization, ed. G. Shipley et al. (Cambridge University Press, 2006).
C. Mee and A. Spawforth, *Greece* (Oxford Archaeological Guides, 2001).
Oxford Classical Dictionary, 3rd edn., ed. S. Hornblower and A. Spawforth (Oxford University Press, 1996 and updates).
Oxford Dictionary of the Classical World, by John Roberts (Oxford University Press, 2007) [an abridged reworking of the *OCD*].
Princeton Encyclopedia of Classical Sites, ed. R. Stillwell (Princeton University Press, 1976).

Ancient Sources

i. Texts in Translation

M. Austin, *The Hellenistic World from Alexander to the Roman Conquest*, 2nd edn. (Cambridge University Press, 2006).

S. Burstein, *The Hellenistic Age from the Battle of Ipsos to the Death of Kleopatra VII* (Cambridge University Press, 1985).

M. Crawford and D. Whitehead, *Archaic and Classical Greece: A Selection of Ancient Sources in Translation* (Cambridge University Press, 1983).

M. Dillon and L. Garland, *Ancient Greece: Social and Historical Documents from Archaic Times to the Death of Socrates* (Routledge, 1994).

C. W. Fornara, *Archaic Times to the End of the Peloponnesian War*, 2nd edn. (Cambridge University Press, 1983).

P. Harding, *From the End of the Peloponnesian War to the Battle of Ipsus* (Cambridge University Press, 1985).

P. Rhodes, *The Greek City States: A Sourcebook*, 2nd edn. (Cambridge University Press, 2007).

ii. Archaeology, Language

S. E. Alcock and R. Osborne (eds.), *Classical Archaeology* (Blackwell, 2007).

A.-Ph. Christidis (ed.), *A History of Ancient Greek: From the Beginnings to Late Antiquity* (Cambridge University Press, 2007).

Modern Works

i. One-volume Overviews

J. Boardman, J. Griffin, and O. Murray (eds.), *The Oxford History of the Classical World* (Oxford University Press, 1986).

R. Browning (ed.), *The Greek World: Classical, Byzantine and Modern* (Thames & Hudson, 1985).

P. Cartledge (ed.), *The Cambridge Illustrated History of Ancient Greece*, rev. edn., paperback (Cambridge University Press, 2002).

C. Freeman, *Egypt, Greece and Rome: Civilizations of the Ancient Mediterranean*, 2nd edn. (Oxford University Press, 2004), esp. chs. 8–19.

C. Higgins, *It's All Greek To Me: From Homer to the Hippocratic Oath: How Ancient Greece Has Shaped our World* (Short Books, 2008).

P. Levi, *Atlas of the Greek World* (Phaidon, 1980).

ii. Historiography

M. Crawford (ed.), *Sources for Ancient History* (Cambridge University Press, 1983).

C. Fornara, *The Nature of History in Ancient Greece and Rome* (University of California Press, 1983).

J. Marincola (ed.), *A Companion to Greek and Roman Historiography*, 2 vols. (Blackwell, 2007).

Periods

Prehistory, General

O. Dickinson, *The Aegean Bronze Age* (Cambridge University Press, 1994).

C. Renfrew, *The Emergence of Civilisation: The Cyclades and the Aegean in the Third Millennium B.C.* (Cambridge University Press, 1972).

Protohistory and Early History to 500

J. Boardman, *The Greeks Overseas: Their Early Colonies and Trade*, 4th edn. (Thames & Hudson, 1999).

A. R. Burn, *The Lyric Age of Greece* (Methuen, 1960; rev. edn. 1978).

O. Dickinson, *The Aegean from Bronze Age to Iron Age* (Routledge, 2006).

See also Murray 1993, Osborne 2009, Hall 2007, Desborough 1972, Coldstream 2004, and Jeffery 1976, below.

Monographs Organized Chronologically, Archaic To Hellenistic

Fontana (Glasgow) series (Oswyn Murray, ed.)

O. Murray, *Early Greece*, 2nd edn. (1993).

J. K. Davies, *Democracy and Classical Greece*, 2nd edn. (1993).

F. W. Walbank, *Hellenistic Greece*, 2nd edn. (1992).

Methuen/Routledge (London) series (Fergus Millar, ed.)

R. Osborne, *Greece in the Making, 1200–480 BC*, 2nd edn. (2009).

S. Hornblower, *The Greek World, 479–323 BC*, 4th edn. (2011).

G. Shipley, *The Greek World after Alexander, 323–30 BC* (2000).

B. Blackwell (Oxford) series

J. Hall, *A History of the Archaic Greek World, ca. 1200–479 BC* (2007).

P. Rhodes, *A History of the Classical Greek World 478–323 BC*, 2nd edn. (2010).

R. Malcolm Errington, *A History of the Hellenistic World 323–30 BC* (2008).

E. Benn (London) series

V. Desborough, *The Greek Dark Ages* (1972).

N. Coldstream, *Geometric Greece* (1977; rev. edn. Routledge, 2004).

L. H. Jeffery, *Archaic Greece: The City States 700–500 BC* (1976).

Cities (See also I.1, Reference, above)

Chapter 1. Introduction

M. H. Hansen, *Polis: An Introduction to the Ancient Greek City-State* (Oxford University Press, 2006).

M. H. Hansen and T. H. Nielsen (eds.), *An Inventory of Archaic and Classical Poleis* (Oxford University Press, 2004).

Chapter 2. Cnossos

A. Brown, *Arthur Evans and the Palace of Minos* (Ashmolean Museum, Oxford, 1993).

G. Cadogan, E. Hatzaki, and A. Vasilakis (eds.), *Knossos: Palace, City, State* (BSA Studies 12, 2004).

J. Chadwick, *The Decipherment of Linear B* (Cambridge University Press, first edn. 1958; latest rev. edn. 1990).

L. Fitton, *The Minoans* (British Museum Press, 2002).

H. Morales, *Classical Mythology: A Very Short Introduction* (Oxford University Press, 2007).

http://www.channel4.com/history/microsites/H/history/ i-m/minoans01.html

Note: The British School at Athens maintains a permanent Stratigraphic Museum at Cnossos, which complements the Greek Herakleion Museum.

Chapter 3. Mycenae

J. Chadwick, *The Decipherment of Linear B* (Cambridge University Press, first edn. 1958; latest rev. edn. 1990).

J. Chadwick, *The Mycenaean World* (Cambridge University Press, 1976).

C. Gere, *The Tomb of Agamemnon: Mycenae and the Search for a Hero* (Profile Books, 2006).

M. Ventris and J. Chadwick, *Documents in Mycenaean Greek* (Cambridge University Press, first edn. 1956; rev. edn. 1973).

Note: Excavations at Mycenae have been undertaken by both the British School and Greek archaeologists since Heinrich Schliemann's less than scholarly excavations in the 1870s.

Chapter 4. Argos

R. A. Tomlinson, *Argos and the Argolid* (Routledge, 1972).

Note: Excavations by the French School of Archaeology at Athens are published in the *Bulletin de Correspondance Hellénique*.

Chapter 5. Miletus

E. Akurgal, *Ancient Civilizations and Ruins of Turkey: From Prehistoric Times until the End of the Roman Empire*, 3rd edn. (Mobil Oil Türk, Istanbul, 1973).

K. Freeman, *Greek City-States* (Macdonald, 1950), 127–79.

A. M. Greaves, *Miletos: A History* (Routledge, 2002).

Chapter 6. Massalia

M. Clavel-Lévêque, *Marseille Grecque: La Dynamique d'un impérialisme marchand* (Jeanne Laffitte, Marseille, 1977).

K. Freeman, *Greek City-States* (Macdonald, 1950), 233–49.

A. Hermary, 'The Greeks in Marseilles and the Western Mediterranean', in V. Karageorghis (ed.), *The Greeks Beyond the Aegean: From Marseilles to Bactria* (A. G. Leventis Foundation, Nicosia, 2004), 59–77.

B. B. Shefton, 'Massalia and Colonization in the North-Western Mediterranean', in G. R. Tsetskhladze and F. De Angelis (eds.), *The Archaeology of Greek Colonisation: Essays Dedicated to Sir John Boardman* (Oxbow Books, 1994), ch. 5.

Chapter 7. Sparta

P. Cartledge, *The Spartans: An Epic History*, 2nd edn. (Pan Macmillan & Vintage, 2003).

P. Cartledge, *Sparta and Lakonia: A Regional History 1300–362 BC*, new edn. (Routledge, 2002).

P. Cartledge and A. Spawforth, *Hellenistic and Roman Sparta: A Tale of Two Cities*, rev. edn. (Routledge, 2002).

R. M. Dawkins (ed.), *Artemis Orthia* (*Journal of Hellenic Studies*, Supp. V, 1929).

Note: The British School at Athens, in collaboration with the Hellenic Ephorate of Prehistoric and Classical Antiquities based in Sparta, has recently recommenced excavations at the Spartan acropolis, where it first excavated in 1906. Results are normally published in the *Annual of the British School at Athens* and its supplements.

Chapter 8. Athens

J. M. Camp II (ed.), *The Athenian Agora: A Guide to the Excavation and the Museum*, 4th edn. (American School of Classical Studies, Athens, 1990).

J. M. Camp II, *The Athenian Agora: Excavations in the Heart of Classical Athens* (Thames & Hudson, 1986 and rev. repr.).

J. M. Camp II, *The Archaeology of Athens* (Yale University Press, 2004).

J. M. Hurwit, *The Athenian Acropolis: History, Mythology and Archaeology from the Neolithic Era to the Present* (Cambridge University Press, 1999).

L. Parlama and N. Ch. Stampolidis (eds.), *The City Beneath the City: Antiquities from the Metropolitan Railway Excavations*

(Catalogue, exhibition at N. P. Goulandris Foundation
Museum for Cycladic Art, Athens, 2000).

Note: Official Greek excavation of Athens began under the
auspices of the Archaeological Society (founded 1837). The Society
still flourishes and excavates, but most archaeological projects in
Athens and Attica are now conducted under the auspices of the
Greek Archaeological Service, a branch of the Ministry of Culture.
The American School of Classical Studies has excavated in the
Agora since 1931 and publishes both a monograph series and an
invaluable, general reader-friendly series entitled 'Agora Picture
Books'.

Chapter 9. Syracuse

K. J. Dover, *The Greeks* (Oxford University Press, 1980), ch. 2.

M. I. Finley, *Ancient Sicily to the Arab Conquest*, 2nd edn. (Chatto
& Windus, 1979).

B. Daix Wescoat (ed.), *Syracuse, the Fairest Greek City: Ancient
Art from the Museo Archeologico Regionale 'Paolo Orsi'*
(University of Pennsylvania Press, 1995).

R. Wilson, *Sicily under the Roman Empire* (Aris & Phillips, 1990).

Chapter 10. Thebes

V. Aravantinos, *The Archaeological Museum of Thebes* (John S.
Latsis Foundation, 2011).

J. Buckler, *The Theban Hegemony, 371–362 B.C.* (Harvard
University Press, 1980).

K. Demakopoulou and D. Konsola, *Archaeological Museum of
Thebes* (Athens, 1981).

Chapter 11. Alexandria

J.-Y. Empereur, *Alexandria: Past, Present and Future* (French
original 2001; Thames & Hudson, 2002).

M. Haag, *Alexandria: City of Memory* (Yale University
Press, 2004).

P. Leriche, 'The Greeks in the Orient: From Syria to Bactria', in V.
Karageorghis (ed.), *The Greeks Beyond the Aegean: From*

Marseilles to Bactria (A. G. Leventis Foundation, Nicosia, 2004), 78–128.

J. McKenzie, *The Architecture of Alexandria and Egypt 300 BC–AD 700* (Yale University Press, 2007).

J. Pollard and H. Reid, *The Rise and Fall of Alexandria: Birthplace of the Modern World* (Viking Penguin, 2006; Penguin Books, 2007).

Chapter 12. Byzantion

E. Akurgal, *Ancient Civilizations and Ruins of Turkey: From Prehistoric Times until the End of the Roman Empire*, 3rd edn. (Mobil Oil Türk, Istanbul, 1973), s.v. 'Byzantium'.

K. Freeman, *Greek City-States* (Macdonald, 1950), 251–62.

Appendix. The Panhellenic Sanctuaries
Olympia

M. I. Finley and H. W. Pleket, *The Olympic Games: The First Thousand Years* (Chatto & Windus, 1976).

J. J. Herrmann, Jr. and C. Kondoleon, *Games for the Gods: The Greek Athlete and the Olympic Spirit* (Museum of Fine Arts, Boston, 2004).

T. Measham, E. Spathari, and P. Donnelly, *1000 Years of the Olympic Games: Treasures of Ancient Greece* (Hellenic Ministry of Culture, Athens, & Powerhouse Museum, Sydney, 2000).

J. Swaddling, *The Ancient Olympic Games*, new edn. (British Museum, 1999 and repr.).

Note: The German Archaeological Institute (DAI) at Athens has been excavating at Olympia since 1876 and publishes two scholarly series, *Olympia-Bericht* and *Olympische Forschungen*. In connection with the Munich Olympics of 1972 the DAI published a scholarly exhibition catalogue: *100 Jahre deutsche Ausgrabung in Olympia*, ed. B. Fellmann and H. Scheyhing (Prestel-Verlag, Munich).

Delphi

B. Chr. Petracos, *Delphi* (Hesperos, Athens, 1971).

The *Wikipedia* entry 'Delphi' has, unusually, useful links.

Note: The French School of Archaeology at Athens has been excavating at Delphi since 1893 and publishes a scholarly series, with Supplementary volumes, entitled *Études Delphiques*.

Chronology

(All dates down to 508/7 are approximate or/and traditional.)

(B)CE = *(Before) Common Era*

BCE

Bronze Age

3000 (to 1000) Minoan (Cretan) civilization

1600 (to 1150) Mycenaean period

1400 Destruction of Cnossos

1250 Destruction of Troy

Early Iron Age

1100 (to 700) Era of Migrations (Dorian migration, Asia Minor settlement, beginnings of Western colonization)

Archaic Age

776 Foundation of Olympic Games

750 Greek alphabet invented, Euboeans settle Ischia and Cumae

735-715 Sparta conquers Messenia

733 Foundation of Syracuse

700 Homer, Hesiod

700 Introduction of hoplite fighting

688/657 Foundation of Byzantion

669 Battle of Hysiae: Argos defeats Sparta

620 Draco's laws at Athens

600 Foundation of Massalia, Thales of Miletus, development of trireme, invention of coinage

594 Solon's laws at Athens

550 Achaemenid Persian empire founded

546 Cyrus (II 'the Great') of Persia defeats Croesus of Lydia

545 (to 510) Tyranny at Athens of Peisistratus and son Hippias

508/7 Cleisthenes introduces Democratic reforms at Athens

505 Sparta's Peloponnesian League formed

Classical Age

499 (to 494) Ionian Revolt: rebellion against Persia of Ionian Greeks and other, Greek and non-Greek subjects

490 Battle of Marathon: Athens and Plataea defeat Persian invaders

480 (to 479) Second Persian invasion, under Xerxes, defeated: Salamis 480, Plataea 479

480 Battle of Himera: Sicilian Greeks under Gelon defeat Carthaginians

478 (to 404) Athens founds anti-Persian Delian League

474 Hieron I of Syracuse defeats Etruscans at Cumae

466 End of tyranny, beginning of Democracy at Syracuse

462 Further Democratic reforms at Athens: Ephialtes and Pericles

460 (to 446) 'First' Peloponnesian War: Sparta and allies vs Athens and allies

449 Peace of Callias (between Athens and Persia; authenticity disputed)

447 Thebes defeats Athens, establishes Oligarchic federal state; Parthenon begun (completed 432)

446 Thirty Years' Truce between Sparta and Athens (broken 431)

431 (to 404, with interruptions) Atheno-Peloponnesian War

421 (to 414) Peace of Nicias

418 Battle of Mantinea: Spartan victory

415 (to 413) Athenian expedition to Sicily: Syracusan victory

405 Dionysius I, tyrant at Syracuse

404 Sparta, with Persian aid, wins Atheno-Peloponnesian War

404 (to 371) Spartan hegemony

401 (to 400) Expedition of the '10,000' to Asia

395 (to 386) Corinthian War: Sparta defeats Quadruple Alliance (Athens, Boeotia, Argos, Corinth)

386 King's Peace: sponsored by Artaxerxes II of Persia and Agesilaus II of Sparta

385 Plato founds Academy

378 (to 338) Athens founds anti-Spartan Second Sea-League,
    Thebes a founder-member
371 Battle of Leuctra: Thebans defeat Spartans.
    Theban ascendancy in mainland Greece (to 362)
367 Death of Dionysius I of Syracuse
366 End of Sparta's Peloponnesian League
362 Second Battle of Mantinea: Theban victory, death of
    Epaminondas; Common Peace renewed
359 Accession of Philip II of Macedon
356 (to 346) Third Sacred War: Phocians vs Philip
346 Peace of Philocrates
338 Battle of Chaeronea, foundation of League of Corinth
336 Murder of Philip II, accession of Alexander ('the Great')
336 (to 323) Reign of Alexander
335 Alexander orders destruction of Thebes.
    Aristotle founds Lyceum at Athens.
    Timoleon dies at Syracuse
334 Alexander invades Persian empire
331 Foundation of Alexandria in Egypt, Battle of Gaugamela
330 End of Achaemenid Persian empire
323 (to 322) Failed revolt of Greeks against Macedon
322 Deaths of Demosthenes and Aristotle.
    Termination of Athenian democracy

Hellenistic Age

301 Battle of Ipsus, death of Antigonus founder of Antigonid
    dynasty of Greece
300 Zeno founds Stoic school
283 Death of Ptolemy I, founder of Ptolemaic dynasty of Egypt
    and of Museum and Library at new capital, Alexandria
281 Seleucus I, founder of Seleucid dynasty of Asia,
    assassinated; Achaean League refounded
263 Eumenes I succeeds Philetaerus as ruler of Pergamum
    kingdom
244 (to 241) Agis IV king at Sparta
238 (to 227) War of Attalus I of Pergamum for mastery of Asia
    Minor
235 (to 222) Cleomenes III king at Sparta
224 (to 222) Antigonus III invades Peloponnese, founds
    Hellenic League
223 (to 187) Antiochus III succeeds Seleucus III
222 Battle of Sellasia: Antigonus III defeats Sparta

221 (to 179) Philip V succeeds Antigonus III

215 Alliance of Philip V and Hannibal of Carthage

211 Alliance between Aetolia and Rome: First Macedonian War
     (to 205); Rome sacks Syracuse

200 (to 197) Second Macedonian War

196 Rome declares Greece 'Free'

194 Rome abandons Greece

192 (to 188) Syrian War of Rome against Antiochus III

171 (to 168) Third Macedonian War

168 Battle of Pydna, end of Antigonid dynasty

148 Macedonia becomes Roman province

147 (to 146) Achaean (League) rising against Rome

Late Roman Republic

146 Sack of Corinth, Achaea becomes Roman protectorate

133 Attalus III of Pergamum bequeaths kingdom to Rome
     (becomes Roman province of Asia)

86 Roman general Sulla sacks Athens

31 Battle of Actium: Octavian defeats Cleopatra and Antony

Early Roman Empire

27 (to CE 14) Octavian/Augustus reigns as First Roman
     Emperor

CE

66–7 Roman Emperor Nero tours Greece, 'wins' at Olympics

117–38 Reign of Emperor Hadrian

267 Heruli sack Athens and Sparta

Byzantine Age

324 Foundation (8 November) of Constantinople
     (refoundation of Byzantion) by Emperor Constantine

330 Dedication (11 May) of Constantinople

395 Emperor Theodosius I orders termination of all non-
     Christian religious worship, such as the Olympic Games

529 Emperor Justinian (527–65) orders closure of Greek
     philosophical Schools

1453 Fall of Constantinople to Mehmet II 'the conqueror',
     Sultan of the Ottoman Turks

Modern Times

1952 'Linear B' deciphered as earliest Greek

2004 M. H. Hansen and T. H. Nielsen (Copenhagen Polis Project) publish *An Inventory of Archaic and Classical Poleis*.

Who's Who

(All dates BCE unless otherwise stated.)

AESCHYLUS c.525–456, Athenian tragedian, said to have written ninety plays, seven surviving (or six, if *Prometheus Bound* is not his)

AGAMEMNON King of Mycenae, commander-in-chief of the Greek expedition against Troy, represented ambivalently by Homer; his murder forms the subject of first play in the *Oresteia* trilogy of Aeschylus, 458

AGESILAUS II co-king of Sparta c.400–360, for a time one of the most powerful figures in mainland Greece but presided over Sparta's decline and fall

ALCIBIADES c.450–404, ward of Pericles and most brilliant if most wayward of his successors, disgraced by treachery, rehabilitated, disgraced again

ALEXANDER THE GREAT born 356, pupil of Aristotle c.343, reigned 336–323; assumed father Philip II's role and completed conquest of Persian empire before early death at Babylon prevented consolidation of a new imperial system

ANAXIMANDER c. first half sixth century, Milesian natural philosopher in line of Thales, conceived of universe as a cosmos in balance

ANTALCIDAS   Spartan general and diplomat, eponym of Peace with Persia in 386 (see Glossary, **King's Peace**)

ANTIPHON   Athenian oligarchic politician, rhetorician, and perhaps philosopher, mastermind of 411 anti-democratic coup but executed for treason

APOLLO   twin of Artemis, especially associated with Delphi and music (and other arts); divine patron of colonization

ARCHIMEDES   *c.*287–212, inventor, especially mathematical, and astronomer, died fighting Romans in defence of his native Syracuse

ARISTIDES   *c.*525–467, Athenian nicknamed 'the Just', because famed for the equity of his original assessment (478/7) of tribute in cash or kind for allies of Athens in Delian League

ARISTOPHANES   *c.*445–385, author of over forty comedies, eleven extant, both master of political Old Comedy (e.g. *Birds*, 414) and inaugurator of Middle Comedy of manners (e.g. *Wealth*, 388)

ARISTOTLE   384–322, originally of Stageira (north Greece), son of court physician to Philip of Macedon's father, pupil of Plato, teacher of Alexander, founded own Lyceum School *c.*335; some 500 titles known, thirty treatises extant, especially biological, zoological and political (esp. *Politics*)

ARTEMIS   twin of Apollo, goddess of hunting and wild nature, associated with transition from girlhood to womanhood

ASPASIA   of Miletus, but famous or notorious for being partner of Pericles, whom she was forbidden to marry by Pericles's own Athenian citizenship law of 451; had son with Pericles also called Pericles, who was made a special grant of citizenship following the deaths in the Great Plague of Pericles's two Athenian sons by his only legal marriage

ATHENA   Olympian goddess daughter of Zeus, who gave birth to her through his cranium; associated especially with war and crafts; patron deity of both Athens and Sparta

BACCHYLIDES   *c.*510–450, of Ceos, relative of Simonides, lyric poet of victory odes and **dithyrambs** (see Glossary)

CALLICRATES   co-architect of Parthenon, also worked on Nike (Victory) temple on Athenian acropolis

CALLIMACHUS   third century, scholar-poet originally from Cyrene, produced first catalogue of Alexandria Royal Library

CALLISTHENES   *c.*380–327, of Olynthus (destroyed by Philip 348), kinsman and co-author of Aristotle, official historian of Alexander, but executed by him for alleged treason

CHILON   mid-sixth century. Spartan ephor, sometimes included in lists of Seven Sages

CIMON   *c.*510–450, son of Miltiades of Marathon, Athenian politician and general, mainly responsible for early development of Delian League, fell out with Pericles over policy towards Persia (aggressive) and Sparta (pacific)

CLEISTHENES   Athenian aristocrat, *c.*565–505, maternal grandson of a tyrant of Sicyon, credited—or debited—with founding the Athenian democracy 508/7

CLEON   leading Athenian politician in succession to Pericles, cordially detested by Thucydides (whose exile he was probably responsible for) and savagely lampooned by Aristophanes (esp. in *Knights*, 424)

CLEOPATRA   69–30, Cleopatra VII, last of the Graeco-Macedonian Ptolemies to rule Egypt following Alexander's conquest, defeated with Antony by Octavian/Augustus at Actium in 31, committed suicide

CRITIAS   *c.*460–403, older relative of Plato, leader of pro-Spartan junta of Thirty Tyrants, wrote works in praise of Sparta in both verse and prose

CROESUS   proverbially wealthy ('rich as Croesus') king of Lydia, reigned *c.*560–546, philhellenic ruler of Greek cities, including Ephesus (whose Artemis temple he adorned), defeated by Cyrus the Great

CYRUS THE GREAT   Cyrus II, Great King of Persia *c.*550–529, founder of Achaemenid Empire, liberator of Jews from Babylon

DARIUS I   Great King of Persia *c.*520–486, second founder of Achaemenid Empire, quelled Ionian Revolt 499–494 but failed at Marathon, 490

DEMOCRITUS *c.*460–370, of Abdera, wrote ethical, mathematical, and musical treatises, but most famous for his 'atomist' theory of physical universe

DEMOSTHENES 384–322, Athenian politician and forensic orator of genius, led Athenian and Greek resistance to Philip and Alexander of Macedon, ultimately without success

DIONYSIUS I tyrant of Syracuse 405–367, kept Greek Sicily free of Carthaginian control, patron of Plato, winner of crown for tragedy at Athens

DIONYSUS god of illusion and ecstasy, especially through wine and drama

DRACO floruit *c.*620, author of earliest Athenian laws, later—unfairly—believed to have been 'written in blood', i.e. to stipulate capital punishment for all or most defined crimes

EPAMINONDAS died 362, Theban general and (Pythagorean) philosopher, most famous for defeating Sparta, 371 and 362, and enabling foundation of Messene and Megalopolis

EPHIALTES assassinated 461, opponent of Cimon, principal author of democratic reforms of 462/1 maintained and developed by Pericles

ERATOSTHENES *c.*275–195, like Callimachus originally from Cyrene but made his name at Alexandria, multi-talented chronographer, literary critic, and geographer

EUCLID floruit 295 (reign of **Ptolemy I**) at Alexandria, mathematician and astronomer, his thirteen books of *Elements* (plane geometry, theory of numbers, stereometry) have remained foundational

EURIPIDES *c.*485–406, tragedian, nineteen of whose *c.*80 attributed plays survive, much ridiculed by comic poets in lifetime but the most popular of the Big Three tragedians after his death, died at Pella, capital of Macedon, where he had written *Bacchae*

GELON tyrant of Syracuse 485–478, defeated Carthaginian invasion at Himera, 480, allegedly on same day as battle of Salamis

GORGIAS *c.*483–375, of Leontini on Sicily, one of four 'ancient Sophists', charmed Athenian Assembly 427, influential teacher and exponent of rhetoric

HARMODIUS   junior beloved of Aristogiton with whom he killed brother of Athenian tyrant Hippias; the pair were the first to receive official honorific statues in the Athenian Agora

HECATAEUS OF MILETUS   floruit *c.*500, politician and geographical historian, author of a *Journey Round the World*, to whom Herodotus was much indebted

HERA   sister-wife of Zeus, associated with human married life; patron deity of Argos

HERODOTUS   *c.*484–425, of Halicarnassus, historian, in exile became citizen of Thurii

HESIOD   floruit *c.*700, didactic poet, author of *Works and Days* and *Theogony*

HIERON I   tyrant of Syracuse 478–467, in succession to Gelon, defeated Etruscans at Cumae, 474, patron of Simonides and Pindar

HIPPIAS   (i) of Athens, tyrant 527–510 in succession to father Pisistratus; (ii) of Elis, later fifth century, ancient Sophist and polymath, e.g. credited with fixing date of first Olympiad

HIPPOCRATES OF COS   *c.*460–380, founder of medical school, attributed with sixty treatises comprising the 'Hippocratic Corpus'

HIPPODAMUS   fifth century, of Miletus, townplanner and utopian political philosopher, redesigned Piraeus and designed new city of Rhodes on orthogonal 'Hippodamian' plan

HOMER   claimed as a native son by many Ionian cities, 'blind Homer' may or may not have flourished in the eighth century and been responsible for combining and developing long oral traditions into the two monumental epic poems that bear his name

ICTINUS   co-architect of Parthenon, also credited with Hall of Initiation at Eleusis and Apollo's temple at Bassae

LEONIDAS I   co-king of Sparta, died heroically at Thermopylae 480

LYCURGUS   of Sparta, possibly mythical lawgiver credited with establishing all main components of Sparta's military, social, and political regime, but laws were all unwritten

LYSANDER   died Haliartus 395, Spartan admiral, key player in Sparta's Peloponnesian War victory, but clashed with former beloved **Agesilaus** over post-War policy

LYSIAS son of Cephalus, an immigrant from Syracuse; one of the ten canonical 'Attic Orators' but a **metic** (see Glossary) never an Athenian citizen, despite active participation in democratic resistance to **Thirty Tyrants** (see Glossary)

LYSIPPUS fourth century, of Sicyon, hugely prolific sculptor most famed for portraits of Alexander

MAUSOLUS hellenized Carian, sub-satrap of Persian province of Caria 377–353/2, based on Greek Halicarnassus, where his sister-widow built for him the original Mausoleum embellished by leading Greek sculptors (see **Scopas**)

MENANDER *c*.342–292, principal author of New Comedy, famed for super-realism of characterization, pupil of Theophrastus

MILTIADES *c*.550–489, Athenian general whose strategy carried the Battle of Marathon, but earlier a tyrant in the Thracian Chersonese and vassal of Persia

MYRON floruit mid-fifth century, Athenian sculptor in bronze best known for his *Discus-thrower* (Roman copies only survive)

NICIAS *c*.470–413, hugely wealthy slave-owning Athenian politician and general, defeated and killed on expedition to Sicily proposed by Alcibiades that he had opposed

PARMENIDES born *c*.515, of Elea in south Italy (hence 'Eleatic' School), expounded his monist philosophy in long hexameter poem

PAUSANIAS OF MAGNESIA floruit 160s–170s CE, religious traveller and antiquarian author of ten-book *Guide to Greece* preserving much lore and fact about Classical Greece

PELOPIDAS *c*.410–364, Theban politician and commander, especially of **Sacred Band** (see Glossary), worked closely with **Epaminondas**

PERICLES *c*.495–429, Athenian democratic statesman, financial expert, and commander, hugely influential *c*.450–430, connected especially with imperial building programme

PHIDIAS *c*.490–430, Athenian sculptor in bronze, marble, and wood embellished with gold and ivory, fashioned cult-statues of Zeus at Olympia and Athena Parthenos at Athens, perhaps responsible for entire sculptural programme of Parthenon, associate of Pericles, disgraced for alleged theft of gold meant for Athena's statue

PHILIP II   ruled Macedon 359–336, conquered most of Greece, planned invasion of Persia but assassinated during daughter's wedding

PHRYNICHUS   floruit *c.*510–476, pioneer Athenian tragedian, fined heavily for his play *Capture of Miletus c.*493 on the grounds that the Athenians found it too distressing

PINDAR   538–448, Theban praise-singer, author of four books of epinician (victory) odes for victors at Olympic, Pythian (Delphi), Isthmian, and Nemean Games

PISISTRATUS   floruit *c.*560–527, three times tyrant of Athens, longest 545–527, promoted lavish public works and Athenocentric cultural and religious programmes

PLATO   *c.*427–347, pupil and disciple of Socrates, founded Academy *c.*385, all known dialogues extant together with some probably falsely attributed

PLUTARCH   *c.*46–120 CE, of Chaeronea, author of over 200 works, of which the seventy-eight *Moral Essays* and fifty biographies (most of them paired Greek–Roman *Lives*) survive

POLYCLITUS   floruit mid-fifth century, of Argos, sculptor and fellow-pupil with Myron

PRAXITELES   floruit 370–330, Athenian sculptor in both marble and bronze, chiefly notorious for first nude Aphrodite cult-statue and liaison with prostitute Phryne ('Toad')

PROTAGORAS   *c.*490–420, of Abdera, 'ancient Sophist', wrote at least two treatises including *On the Gods*, in the preface of which he expressed agnosticism, possibly democratic in politics and author of first constitution for new city of Thurii *c.*445

PTOLEMY I   *c.*367/6–283/2, founder of Ptolemaic kingdom and dynasty of Egypt as 'Successor' of Alexander, probably founded Museum and Library at capital Alexandria, wrote apologetic history

PYTHAGORAS   floruit 530, originally of Samos but settled in exile at Croton, founder of quasi-religious community avoiding animal blood-sacrifice, preoccupied with number-theory and astronomy

PYTHEAS late fourth century, of Massalia, explored waters of northern Europe, including circumnavigation of Britain, possibly as far as Iceland

SAPPHO late seventh century, of Eresus on Lesbos, poet and perhaps pedagogue, her homoerotic lyrics have given us 'Lesbian'

SCOPAS floruit 370–330, of the marble island of Paros, noted for expressiveness of his sculpture, employed on Mausoleum

SIMONIDES c.556–468, of Ceos, relative of Bacchylides, praise-singer most famous for epigrams, e.g. on Athenian dead at Marathon and Spartan dead at Thermopylae

SOCRATES 469–399, Athenian philosopher of unorthodox ethical and religious views and antidemocratic political outlook, satirized by Aristophanes in *Clouds* (423), convicted of impiety 399, never wrote a word of his philosophy

SOLON floruit 594, Athenian poet-politician, chosen Archon to resolve grave crisis, passed laws that mostly superseded those of **Draco**

SOPHOCLES c.496–406, Athenian tragedian and sometime politician, credited with 123 plays of which seven survive (the last, *Oedipus at Colonus*, produced posthumously)

THALES c.625–547, of Miletus, natural philosopher and Sage, alleged to have predicted solar eclipse of 585

THEMISTOCLES c.524–459, Athenian admiral and statesman, guiding spirit of Greek resistance to Persia 480–479, laid foundations of Athens's naval power, ostracized c.471 and ended days as honoured pensioner of Persian Great King

THEOPHRASTUS c.371–287, originally of Eresus, pupil and successor of Aristotle as head of Lyceum, founder of systematic botany, author of collections of laws and customs, and of *Characters*

THRASYBULUS died 389, Athenian democratic statesman and admiral, leader of resistance to **Thirty Tyrants** (see Glossary)

THUCYDIDES c.455–400, historian and general, exiled 424 for failing to preserve Amphipolis, wrote unfinished history of Atheno-Peloponnesian War (431–411)

TIMOLEON *c*.365–334, Corinthian, distinguished himself in Sicily for overthrowing the Syracusan tyranny and defeating a Carthaginian army

XENOPHON *c*.428–354, Athenian, conservative pupil and disciple of Socrates, pro-Spartan, autobiographical soldier of fortune and writer of history, biography, ethics, romance, and technical treatises

XERXES Persian Great King 486–465, son of Darius I whose project of Greek conquest he failed to complete

ZEUS chief of the **Olympians** (see Glossary), brother-husband of Hera, lord of the sky and wielder of the thunderbolt; author of innumerable erotic affairs

Glossary

ACROPOLIS   'high city', citadel

AGÔGÊ   Sparta's state education

AGORA   civic centre, marketplace

ALPHABET, GREEK   borrowed from Phoenician, with addition of signs for vowels, probably in eighth century

AMPHICTIONIC LEAGUE   representatives of mainly central Greek communities (especially Thessalian) chosen to oversee sanctuary of Delphi and Pythian Games; Sparta had a permanent seat representing 'Dorian' Greeks

ARCHAIC AGE   conventionally dated from 750 or 700 to either 500 or 480 BCE, 'Archaic' implying (perhaps falsely) an immaturity by comparison to the **Classical Age**

ARCHON   civic official

ARISTOCRACY   rule (*kratos*) of the so-called best men (*aristoi*)

ATHENO-PELOPONNESIAN WAR   generation-long war between Athens and Sparta and their respective allies (431–404 with intervals), resulting in total victory for Sparta, with Persian aid

ATTICA   home territory of Athens, *c*.1,000 sq. m./ 2,400 sq. km.

CHORÊGUS   Athenian impresario, wealthy citizen required to finance a dramatic chorus for a festival

CHORUS   song, dance, group of singers/dancers (e.g. twelve or fifteen in a tragic chorus at Athens)

CLASSICAL AGE   conventionally dated from either 500 or 480 to 323 BCE (death of Alexander the Great)

COINAGE   stamping with an identifying badge of state a fixed weight of precious metal bullion (gold, silver, electrum—a gold–silver mix) probably invented by non-Greek Lydians late seventh/early sixth century, soon borrowed by Greeks, e.g. Miletus: see 'Greek Measures of Money and Distance', pp. xix–xx

COLONIZATION   conventional but inaccurate term for process of emigration and foundation of entirely new cities/settlements: Ionian migration (eleventh/tenth century), 'colonization' era proper *c*.750–550, and post-Alexander settlement of Middle East and Central Asia

COMEDY   singing and revelry, formally introduced as dramatic form in **Great Dionysia**, 486

DARK AGE   assumed in this book to be a transitional phase between prehistory and early history, roughly from 1100 to 800 BCE (but darkness is in the eye of the beholder, and some areas of the Greek world in this period were markedly lighter—or darker—than others)

DELIAN LEAGUE   imperial alliance dominated by Athens, 478–404

DEME   parish, ward, village of Athens and Attica, 139 in all

DEMOCRACY   literally, sovereign power (*kratos*) of the *Dêmos*

DÊMOS   people, citizen body, common people

DITHYRAMB   a cultic song, perhaps invented by Arion of Lesbos in the late seventh century, sung by a chorus in honour of Dionysus

DORIANS   ethnic division of Greeks, based—as **Ionians**—on dialect and some distinctive religious customs; chief city Sparta (also Cnossos, Mycenae, Argos, Syracuse, Byzantion)

DRACHMA   monetary unit, literally a 'fistful' of 6 obols

ECCLÊSIA   assembly, because attenders were literally 'called out' to participate; later associated with religious assemblies in Christian churches, whence 'ecclesiastical', French 'église'

EPHORS   board of five chief executive officials of Sparta, annually elected by the Assembly by a curious process of shouting; had special oversight of the unique Spartan educational system (**agôgê**)

GREAT DIONYSIA   annual religious festival at Athens in honour of Dionysus, scene of tragedy, comedy, and satyr-drama

HELLENISTIC AGE   conventionally dated from death of Alexander, 323, to death of Cleopatra, 30 BCE; not to be confused with 'Hellenic' = Greek

HELOT   native Greek serf-like subject of Sparta, both in Laconia and Messenia

HETAERA   expensive prostitute, courtesan

HOPLITE   heavily armed Greek infantryman

HYBRIS   (**hubris**) violation of another's status with malevolent intent

IONIANS   ethnic division of Greeks, based—as **Dorians**—on dialect and some distinctive religious customs, took name from Ion son of Apollo; chief city Athens (also Miletus, Massalia)

KING'S PEACE   concluded in 386, and so called after Persian Great King Artaxerxes II, but alternatively known as the Peace of **Antalcidas** (see Who's Who); between them, Persia and Sparta carved up the Aegean Greek world

KOINÊ   'common' sc. language, the universal form of Greek developed after Alexander the Great's time, based chiefly on the Athenian local dialect

LACEDAEMÔN   (i) official name of polis of Sparta; (ii) territory of Sparta, *c.*3,000 sq. m./8,000 sq. km.

LOGOS   word, speech, reason, account

MEDES   Iranian people related to and regularly confused with Persians; 'medism', a strictly inaccurate Greek term for traitorous collaboration with the Persians against Greek interests

METIC   more or less permanently resident alien, subject to a monthly poll-tax

MYSTAE   initiates, e.g. in Eleusinian Mysteries

OBOL   monetary unit, derived from *obelos,* 'spit'

OIKOS household or extended family, including slaves, animals, and other property; also house (including that of a god or goddess)

OLIGARCHY rule (*archê*) of the (wealthy) few (*oligoi*)

OLYMPIA sanctuary of Olympian Zeus, site of quadrennial Games, first in 776 BCE (as determined by Hippias of Elis)

OLYMPIAD method of time-reckoning according to four-year periods between Olympic Games (first used in third century BCE as historical reckoner, by Timaeus of Sicilian Tauromenium)

OLYMPIANS major twelve gods and goddesses inhabiting peak of Mount Olympus, presided over by **Zeus** (see Who's Who)

OSTRACISM enforced exile from Athens for ten years, decided by counting names of 'candidates' inscribed on *ostraka*, potsherds

PAGANISM a *paganus* (Latin) was a countrydwelling villager, whereas the first Christians were 'townies', so that one term for 'non-Christian' was 'pagan'

PELOPONNESE 'island of Pelops', landmass linked to central Greece by Isthmus of Corinth

PELOPONNESIAN WAR see **Atheno-Peloponnesian War**

PERSIAN EMPIRE *c*.550–330, founded by Cyrus, ended by Alexander

PLATAEA small town in Boeotia near border with Attica, site of decisive land battle of Persian Wars, 479

POLIS city (state, urban centre), citizen-state; usually associated with a *chôra*—countryside, rural territory; whence *politeia*—citizenship, constitution (e.g. democracy)

PYTHIA oracular priestess of Apollo at Delphi

SACRED BAND crack Theban infantry force of 300, consisting of 150 homosexual pairs, founded 378

SATRAP viceroy of province of the Persian Empire

SATYR-DRAMA humorous drama with satyrs (goat-man mythical familiars of Dionysus) as chorus, presented by tragedians at Athens as a compulsory addition to their trilogies

SEVEN SAGES   a body of varying composition, including Chilon, Solon, Thales

STADION   one length of athletic racetrack, *c*.200 metres

STASIS   a 'standing' apart, so faction, civil war

SYNOECISM   'housing-together' (see *oikos*), so unification of villages to form centralized political community

TALENT   measure of weight and monetary value, originally Babylonian; equals 6,000 drachmas

THEBES   chief *polis* of the Boeotians

THERMOPYLAE   'Hot Gates', pass in north-central Greece, site of unsuccessful but heroic Greek resistance, led by Leonidas of Sparta, to Persian land invasion, 480

THIRTY TYRANTS   self-appointed *dunasteia* (junta) of extreme oligarchs, led by Critias, ruled Athens brutally 404–403, murdering as many as 1,000; defeated by democratic coalition led by Thrasybulus

TRIREME   three-banked, oared warship, 170 rowers

TYRANT   illegitimate, absolute ruler, holding power through usurpation and/or force

Index

H

Hadrian 125
Halicarnassus 24, 59
  Mausoleum at 91
Hammurabi of Babylon 7
Hansen, M. H. 4
Hecataeus of Miletus 36
Helen of Sparta (and Troy) 15, 19, 51, 52
Hellas (Greek world), Hellenes 23, 30, 63, 79, 83, 131
hellenicity, hellenism 3, 23, 32, 87, 95, 103, 123
Hellenistic world 5, 110, 111, 114–6
Hellespont 19, 33, 45, 69, 78, 103, 117–9, 121
Helot revolts 54, 58, 59
Helots 54, 55, 57, 60, 61, 87, 98
Hera 25–6, 119, 122; *see also* Argive Heraeum
Heracles 53, 93
Herodotus 3, 4, 7, 9, 22, 24–6, 32, 39, 44, 48, 50, 52, 59; *see also* historiography, history
heroes, hero-worship 17, 21, 29, 51, 53, 55–7, 65, 69, 71, 74, 83, 87, 110
Hesiod 21, 94
Hieron, tyrant of Syracuse 19, 86–8
Himera, battle 85, 86
Hippias, tyrant of Athens 67
Hippocrates of Cos 74
Hippodamus of Miletus 37, 64
historiography, history 1, 2, 7, 9, 10, 13, 19, 32, 41, 43, 51, 60, 61, 64–8, 73, 77, 81, 85, 88, 99, 101, 112
Hittites 16
Homer, Homeric epics 11, 14–17, 19–21, 23, 29, 32, 83
homosexuality 98
hoplites (heavy infantry) 29, 46, 56, 69, 96
Horace 124, 126

horses 84, 87, 135
household, housing 63
Hyacinthia 58
Hyacinthus 52
Hypatia 116
Hysiae, battle 28, 54

I

Ictinus, architect 74
imperialism 38
impiety 78
India 106
Iolcus (Volos) 16
Ionia, Ionians 30–2, 38–40, 43, 44, 48, 66, 69, 72, 77, 89, 119
Ionic dialect and culture 20, 25, 31
iron 20, 28, 48, 87
islands 4, 5, 7, 9, 11–14, 19, 20, 24, 26, 32, 37, 43, 47, 48, 50, 60, 72–4, 81, 83–6, 89, 92, 101, 119, 121, 123, 130, 142
Istanbul 5, 118, 135

J

Jews 107
Julian the Apostate 125
justice, *see* laws, lawcourts
Justinian 130

K

kings, kingship 28, 39, 56, 57, 120
  worship of 106
King's Peace 97, 121

L

Laconia 51, 55
land 13, 24, 26, 29, 37, 42, 44, 45, 54, 55, 57, 59, 60, 63, 71, 80, 82, 83, 91, 107, 109, 118

X

Z

Expand your collection of
VERY SHORT INTRODUCTIONS

ANCIENT EGYPT
A Very Short Introduction
Ian Shaw

The ancient Egyptians are an enduring source of fascination – mummies and pyramids, curses and rituals have captured the imagination of generations. We all have a mental picture of ancient Egypt, but is it the right one? How much do we really know about this great civilization?

In this absorbing introduction, Ian Shaw describes how our current ideas about Egypt are based not only on the thrilling discoveries made by early Egyptologists but also on fascinating new kinds of evidence produced by modern scientific and linguistic analyses. He also explores the changing influences on our responses to these finds, through such media as literature, cinema and contemporary art. Each chapter deals with a different aspect of ancient Egypt, from despotic pharaohs to dismembered bodies, and from hieroglyphs to animal-headed gods.

www.oup.com/vsi/

CLASSICAL MYTHOLOGY
A Very Short Introduction
Helen Morales

From Zeus and Europa, to Diana, Pan, and Prometheus, the myths of ancient Greece and Rome seem to exert a timeless power over us. But what do those myths represent, and why are they so enduringly fascinating? This imaginative and stimulating *Very Short Introduction* is a wide-ranging account, examining how classical myths are used and understood in both high art and popular culture, taking the reader from the temples of Crete to skyscrapers in New York, and finding classical myths in a variety of unexpected places: from Arabic poetry and Hollywood films, to psychoanalysis, the bible, and New Age spiritualism.

www.oup.com/vsi

BIBLICAL
ARCHAEOLOGY
A Very Short Introduction
Eric H. Cline

Archaeologist Eric H. Cline here offers a complete overview of
this exciting field. He discusses the early pioneers, the origins of
biblical archaeology as a discipline, and the major controversies
that first prompted explorers to go in search of sites that would
"prove" the Bible. He then surveys some of the most well-known
modern archaeologists, the sites that are essential sources of
knowledge for biblical archaeology, and some of the most
important discoveries that have been made in the last half
century, including the Dead Sea Scrolls and the Tel Dan Stele.

ENGLISH LITERATURE

A Very Short Introduction

Jonathan Bate

Sweeping across two millennia and every literary genre,
acclaimed scholar and biographer Jonathan Bate provides a
dazzling introduction to English Literature. The focus is wide,
shifting from the birth of the novel and the brilliance of English
comedy to the deep Englishness of landscape poetry and the
ethnic diversity of Britain's Nobel literature laureates. It goes on to
provide a more in-depth analysis, with close readings from an
extraordinary scene in King Lear to a war poem by Carol Ann
Duffy, and a series of striking examples of how literary texts
change as they are transmitted from writer to reader.

www.oup.com/vsi

HERODOTUS
A Very Short Introduction
Jennifer T. Roberts

Herodotus: A Very Short Introduction introduces readers to what little is known of Herodotus' life and goes on to discuss all aspects of his work, including his fascination with his origins; his travels; his view of the world in relation to boundaries and their transgressions; and his interest in seeing the world and learning about non-Greek civilizations. We also explore the recurring themes of his work, his beliefs in dreams, oracles, and omens, the prominence of women in his work, and his account of the battles of the Persian Wars.

www.oup.com/vsi

LATE ANTIQUITY
A Very Short Introduction
Gillian Clark

Late antiquity is the period (c.300–c.800) in which barbarian invasions ended Roman Empire in Western Europe by the fifth century and Arab invasions ended Roman rule over the eastern and southern Mediterranean coasts by the seventh century. Asking 'what, where, and when' Gillian Clark presents an introduction to the concept of late antiquity and the events of its time. Not only a period of cultural clashes, political restructurings, and geographical controversies, Clark also demonstrates the sheer richness and diversity of religious life as well as the significant changes to trade, economy, archaeology, and towns. Encapsulating significant developments through vignettes, she reflects upon the period by asking the question 'How much can we recognise in the world of late antiquity?'

MEDIEVAL LITERATURE
A Very Short Introduction
Elaine Treharne

This *Very Short Introduction* provides a compelling account of the emergence of the earliest literature in Britain and Ireland, including English, Welsh, Scottish, Irish, Anglo-Latin and Anglo-Norman. Introducing the reader to some of the greatest poetry, prose and drama ever written, Elaine Treharne discusses the historical and intellectual background to these works, and considers the physical production of the manuscripts and the earliest beginnings of print culture. Covering both well-known texts, such as *Beowulf*, *The Canterbury Tales* and the *Mabinogion*, as well as texts that are much less familiar, such as sermons, saints' lives, lyrics and histories, Treharne discusses major themes such as sin and salvation, kingship and authority, myth and the monstrous, and provides a full, but brief, account of one of the major periods in literary history.

www.oup.com/vsi

PHILOSOPHY IN THE ISLAMIC WORLD
A Very Short Introduction
Peter Adamson

In the history of philosophy, few topics are so relevant to today's cultural and political landscape as philosophy in the Islamic world. Yet, this remains one of the lesser-known philosophical traditions. In this *Very Short Introduction*, Peter Adamson explores the history of philosophy among Muslims, Jews, and Christians living in Islamic lands.

Introducing the main philosophical themes of the Islamic world, Adamson integrates ideas from the Islamic and Abrahamic faiths to consider the broad philosophical questions that continue to invite debate. Drawing on the most recent research in the field, this book challenges the assumption of the cultural decline of philosophy and science in the Islamic world by demonstrating its rich heritage and overlap with other faiths and philosophies.

www.oup.com/vsi